PERGAMON INTERNATIONAL LIBRARY
of Science, Technology, Engineering and Social Studies
The 1000-volume original paperback library in aid of education, industrial training and the enjoyment of leisure
Publisher: Robert Maxwell, M.C.

MARGINS FOR SURVIVAL

Overcoming Political Limits in Steering Technology

Other Titles of Interest

BALASSA, B.
Policy Reform in Developing Countries

COLE, S.
Global Models and the International Economic Order

JOLLY, R.
Disarmament and World Development

LASZLO, E.
The Inner Limits of Mankind: Heretical Reflections on the Predicament of Mankind

LASZLO, E. and BIERMAN, J.
Goals in a Global Community, Volumes 1 and 2

MENON, B. P.
Global Dialogue: The New International Economic Order

PECCEI, A.
The Human Quality

TICKELL, C.
Climatic Change and World Affairs

MARGINS FOR SURVIVAL

Overcoming Political Limits in Steering Technology

by

EDWARD WENK, Jr.

UNIVERSITY OF WASHINGTON, SEATTLE

PERGAMON PRESS

Oxford · New York · Toronto · Sydney · Paris · Frankfurt

U.K.	Pergamon Press Ltd., Headington Hill Hall, Oxford OX3 0BW, England
U.S.A.	Pergamon Press Inc., Maxwell House, Fairview Park, Elmsford, New York 10523, U.S.A.
CANADA	Pergamon of Canada Ltd., Suite 104, 150 Consumers Road, Willowdale, Ontario M2J 1P9, Canada
AUSTRALIA	Pergamon Press (Aust.) Pty. Ltd., P.O. Box 544, Potts Point, N.S.W. 2011, Australia
FRANCE	Pergamon Press SARL, 24 rue des Ecoles, 75240 Paris, Cedex 05, France
FEDERAL REPUBLIC OF GERMANY	Pergamon Press GmbH, 6242 Kronberg-Taunus, Pferdstrasse 1, Federal Republic of Germany

First edition 1979

British Library Cataloguing in Publication Data

Wenk, Edward, Jr.
Margins for survival.—(Pergamon international library).
1. Technology and state 2. Political science—
Decision making 3. Science Policy—
Technology Assessment
I. Title
609 T49.5 78–40932

ISBN 0–08–023373–2 (Hardcover)
ISBN 0–08–023372–4 (Flexicover)

Printed in Great Britain by Biddles Ltd, Guildford, Surrey

Dedication

This book is dedicated to those individuals in the public service who, in their decisions, consider that citizens of the year 2000 are among their valued constituents

Contents

Preface

Over the last 20 years, by the accident of circumstances, I have been in positions close to where policy was being made. I have served as a science and technology advisor to the United States Congress, and I have been on the staffs of three United States Presidents. From these vantage points, I have seen incumbents agonize over choice. Moreover, as the number of decisions, their complexity, and their costs of error increased, and as the issues became more heavily loaded and clouded with technological content, the quality of decision making on the basis of shortfall in intended results seemed to deteriorate.

Presidents and Congressmen wanted to do the right thing. With few, albeit conspicuous, lapses they were devoted to the public interest. Nevertheless, they seemed to be in a vise not of their own making that constrained them politically. Then, subjected to new levels of decision stress, their anxiety rose: over not finding exits from the new predicaments erupting nationally and internationally, over rising heat of conflicts among interest groups, over their own lack of understanding of the situation, over dilemmas in terms of consequences to them personally, and thus over their own inadequacies, frustrations and threats to prestige as national leaders.

Here was a powerful enigma. But what gripped me even more strongly was a trend of increasing dangers that can be summarized only as threats to survival. People may be an endangered species. While it would be easy to classify this feeling as overreaction to a tide of doomsday rhetoric, independent research verified not only the credibility of emerging perils, but also the conspicuously increasing failure to cope, especially to cope politically.

Thus, when I left government for academia, I had an unprecedented opportunity to search for explanations. Moreover, as an optimistic human being given to action, and as a pragmatist conditioned by professional engineering practice and by life experience as policy advisor close to where decisions are made, I wanted to find remedies.

This book is a product of that quest. It represents a distillation of experience in studying, drafting and implementing policy, not so much to prepare a compendium of analytical case studies as to guide an inquiry by readers through abundant and wide-ranging fields of relevant scholarship, particularly to sensitize an awareness of the overarching predicaments toward which technology-intensive public policy must be generated and tuned.

The research concentrated swiftly on one question. Why is the policy apparatus deaf to signals about the future?

Answers to that question amount to a diagnosis of pathologies in hearing and in listening—pathologies of the short run. A theme soon emerged that technological decision making is becoming more political. Caught in the squeeze of short-run pressures for political survival as opposed to the flickering awareness of far more distant threats to human survival, the politician undergoes a heightened state of psychological–emotional stress. Two things then happen. Decisions are made without a balanced consideration of the future in terms of consequences of present action or of inaction. Short-run expediency dominates.

Equally alarming, sustained neglect of the future systematically undermines the decision apparatus itself so as to drain energy, depress inclinations to look ahead and even disable competence to decide.

That is what is so ominous.

Some observers of this scene contend that we are up against limits—limits of nature; limits of human nature; limits of human intellect; or limits to social organization.

In this inquiry we examine the political limits, limits revealed by institutional behavior in the deliberate act of steering technology to produce socially satisfactory outcomes. Phrasing this analysis another way, confrontation with the future is developed in terms of political decision making about the future.

Chapter 1 sets the stage to define our situation, the dimensions of our predicament. Perspective is developed on how technology is intertwined with civilization, has engraved our culture, amplified our political acts and heightened the role of government.

Chapter 2 catalogues unexpected, unprecedented and potentially lethal threats which have in common a base of technological ingredients and which are so neglected that we seem to survive by the skin of our teeth. The way human beings characteristically cope with risk and its management is discussed, including the role of government in affording collective security.

In Chapter 3 we begin to unravel technology not simply as science and engineering but as a tangled network of social processes and institutions involving everyone and creating a new scale of social complexity and interdependence. We also examine why technological decision making has become more political, to the point that the President of the United States, for example, has become systems manager. Dealing with portents of the future is accordingly focused on implications of political choice in generating strategies for collision avoidance.

Chapter 4 spotlights decision malfunctioning. We examine both the role of public policy as a steering mechanism for a fragmented society and the mechanics of deciding. Then we isolate new criteria for choice in terms of political consequences that implicitly if not explicitly shape the future. Because we are obliged to paint such a broad canvas, at this point we try to help the reader by taking stock of implications that the decision apparatus is severely challenged beyond its capabilities, up against its political limits.

In Chapter 5, we get to the heart of the matter: why decision making in the political theatre is so severely stressed as to be vulnerable to pathologies of the short run. And we begin to sense that the political limits stem not from the fundamental precepts or structure of democratic government, but from the contemporary cultural set. Indeed, it would seem that the political apparatus itself is being undermined so it cannot cope with the future. Additional diagnostic tools are then introduced to probe the role of technology assessment as anticipatory protective reaction.

Prescriptions by other observers for dealing with the future are inventoried in Chapter 6, although very few engage the notion of political limits.

Chapter 7 introduces impressionistic evidence to relate cause and effect and to isolate three major features of the present situation:

scarcity of time, scarcity of activists and scarcity of reserves of resources to deal with the future.

In Chapters 8 and 9 a search is begun for remedies, emphasizing the importance of prevention, the need to image the future and the roles of shared information and analysis in anticipatory decision making. Models are suggested by two probing questions: What will happen, if . . .? What can happen, unless . . .? We also deal with the contention that politicians will consider longer term consequences of impetuous action or neglect, mainly when rewarded by people who want them to change. So prescriptions are offered that involve bottom-up rather than top-down response, especially to deal with the most critical task: restoring health to the decision process by a doctrine of anticipation.

Chapter 10 is intended as a forceful reminder that since the problems have global dimensions, so do solutions.

The epilogue, Chapter 11, is a personal statement by the author—that to be alive and free, rational humanism is not enough. To have a future at all, the reader is guided to the often soft-pedaled spiritual dimensions of life; ultimate collective social strategy may hinge on a regenerated moral imperative.

While the author clearly takes full responsibility for the text, salient ideas and interpretations of many individuals are entailed. References are cited wherever the source can be traced, but many of the notions were inevitably seeded by conversations with colleagues and associates, and especially with key figures in government who innocently played a role as teachers. First among these was Hubert H. Humphrey, with whom the author was privileged to work for over 18 years. Senator Humphrey displayed a rare and sensitive perception that the future begins not just today but by yesterday's decision, and that the vision of the future should always be integrated into political choice. What further distinguished this man was his balance between political survival and advocacy of the public interest, his visible demonstration of humanity and integrity. Here was a model of a patriot. Indeed, it was his courageous and often lonely concern for steering technology by public policy that constituted an inspiration and guide for the author's own work and values.

There have been other teachers among political leaders, staff at the

Congressional Research Service, public-spirited citizens and a wide range of philosophers and scholars. Some few deserve special mention in having a conspicuous influence on my outlook and comprehension, albeit unbeknownst to them: Philip H. Abelson, Kenneth E. Boulding, Detlev W. Bronk, Jacques-Yves Cousteau, Emilio Q. Daddario, Karl Deutsch, Hugh Elsbree, John Kenneth Galbraith, J. Huizinga, Milton Katz, Michael Marien, Charles A. Mosher, Don K. Price, Sir Geoffrey Vickers, my family, my students and the six most recent Presidents.

There are also those whose treasured advice and counsel should be explicitly acknowledged for having read and criticized part or all of the manuscript: Giovanni Costigan, Jacques Y. Cousteau, Malcolm Dondi, Amitai Etzioni, John Fobes, Christopher Freeman, Fremont Lyden, Pauline Marston, William Page, Milton Pikarsky, Don K. Price, Thomas Whiston, Gilbert White, Dael Wolfle and Sir Geoffrey Vickers.

No manuscript would ever see the light of day without inspired and dedicated assistance in translating and transforming handwritten cuneiform to typescript. For this enormous task, I thank Carolyn L. Wenk and Heidi Weikert, the latter also for her meticulous aid through all the mechanics of publication. Marion Impola was also an invaluable partner with her talented and perceptive editing of the entire manuscript.

Finally, I want to acknowledge the resources that made this project possible: the University of Washington for its grant of professional leave; the General Electric Foundation for its grant to support requisite research; the Rockefeller Foundation for my appointment as a visiting scholar at the Bellagio Study Center; Harvard University, Woods Hole Oceanographic Institution and the University of Sussex for similar appointments, during which a salubrious environment proved uniquely conducive to collegiate stimulation, thinking and writing. For these acts of generosity and confidence, I am deeply and forever grateful.

Seattle EDWARD WENK, JR.
May, 1978

CHAPTER 1

Introduction

The Precarious Situation

In recent history the end of a century has evoked universal interest in the human condition. We seem compelled to take stock of where we are and especially to speculate on the way ahead. Approach to the year 2000 manifests that same inclination. Books on social directions, for example, that were being published in the United States at the rate of three per year in the 1930s and 18 per year in the 1960s have sharply increased to over 100 in 1975.[(1)]* Even the content of news headlines and of political evangelism reflect a heightened consciousness of the same two questions: Where are we now? Where are we headed? Reformers and concerned citizens venture a third question: Where should we be headed and what should we do?

The reconnaissance of the future by prophets, philosophers, authors of science fiction and system analysts is highly varied in method and in substance. Some portray the collective situation in social, environmental, economic, political or cultural terms, or in rich combination. Others focus on psychological–spiritual qualities of the individual; the openness or the limits of human potential. One might expect imaging the future to be cautious, for uncertainty about what happens next is the only reality. But interpreters are not timid with either their social diagnoses or their prescriptions.

Few are optimists; but optimism is not currently fashionable. Nor is it to be expected by the very nature of social criticism. Spenglerian-type gloom is almost an essential core of facile speculation, and projections of different species and degrees of Hell have always seemed more graphic and entertaining than nominations for paradise. Even

* Numbers refer to references, notes and details at the end of the book.

classical adherents to the Christian faith sketched the future more as Dantesque penalties for unmitigated original sin than as incentives for good behavior.

The optimist–pessimist label, however, is too simplistic in assessing our condition, and singularly unproductive in altering pernicious trends. It is not enough to consider whether people feel in a state of euphoric well-being and hope or in a funk of unfocused anxiety over ultimate disaster. We must also ask, What are the dimensions of the predicament in which humankind finds itself today? What are the specific perils? What is our repertoire of response to survive, not just biologically, but to survive with self-esteem?[(2)] What must be our strategies of collision avoidance? Why does government that has always been accorded collective security as its first responsibility focus more on the urgent rather than the important? Why does it neglect the future in making decisions?

Human beings have always faced challenges to existence, from a strenuous natural environment, self-serving brutality of other people, and self-destructive tendencies of the human psyche. Now, however, we are haunted by new orders of exposure. In occupying and exploiting the entire planet, people may be innocently exhausting some of nature's resilience against insult. Moreover, the technological power exists to debase individual integrity if not to extinguish human society altogether. Such consequences of collective error seem more critical than ever before because they are so grave and potentially irreversible.

At the same time, ideas of progress and belief in the perfectibility of man that have been axiomatic in Western culture for centuries are increasingly questioned and doubted.

Such dramas of the future have been elegantly staged with such titles as: *Freedom in a Rocking Boat: Changing Values in an Unstable Society*; *The Doomsday Book: Can the World Survive?*; *Between Two Ages: America's Role in the Technetronic Era*; *Future Shock*; *Friendly Fascism: A Model for America*; *Limits to Growth*; *This Endangered Planet: Prospects and Proposals for Human Survival*; *Twilight of Authority*; *1984*. Studied word choices by authors are intended to be emotive as well as informative, as indeed they must be, for our feelings are basic instinctive cues to threat and to survival.

These monographs and their bookshelf neighbors deal with five problems: war, poverty, social injustice, ecological instability and dehumanization.[3] While these disasters come in various shades, their contributing causes are distinguished by surprisingly common features; most, incidentally, are sharply transformed from the perceptions of the world widely held one hundred years ago.

The situation is roughly this:

—Technology has demonstrated a capacity to generate great economic wealth, to enhance material standards of living, to improve health and, in the West, to provide a wider range of personal options. Indeed, technology has become intimately symbiotic with processes of civilization. Artifacts become treasured ingredients of Western culture. We have become a knowledge-based society.[4]

—Technology is regarded by both developing and developed nations as the crucible for future economic growth, partly because it has been proven the key to abundance, and partly because economic growth is itself widely heralded as essential to progress. Yet technology has failed to meet its promise as a source of social equity, so that economic disparity between the technologically advanced and the developing world is increasing.

—Technology has locked nations together in one world, for with swift transportation and communication, events anywhere exert effects everywhere.

—The technology of nuclear weapons has generated the risk of annihilation on an unprecedented scale.

—Technology has increasingly intermingled people and nature, and accelerated uncritical consumption of natural resources.

—Now we are discovering that technological initiatives induce capricious, unexpected and unwanted side effects, which frustrate social performance and potentially damage both the human habitat and the human spirit.

—Some of these side effects arise because technologies are usually organized on a project basis, narrowly directed to specific purposes. Resulting fragmentation undermines a congruity of goals and orchestration of participants, generates cross-impacts for innocent bystanders and reduces sensitivity to these externalities.

—The swift pace of technological change no longer matches the response time of human affairs; technical prowess may exceed the pace of social skills, especially our ability to anticipate second-order consequences and take crisis avoidance measures.

—Virtually all public and private institutions are engaged in technological enterprises, and these have become more numerous, varied and interdependent. But they now appear clumsy in relation to the energizing force of the technology they mediate.

—Communication linkages among these institutions, public and private, have become more urgent, complex and demanding; everything seems connected to everything else.

—Because technology acts as an organizing principle to concentrate power and wealth, it plays a political role in our society, accentuating both the distribution of benefits and the selection of beneficiaries.

—Committed to growth in size and in power to influence their environment, individual institutions become ever more self-centered, coasting on momentum of past choices, intent on achieving their narrow objectives, indifferent to costs borne by others in the system.

—Cultures that were previously isolated by geography have been brought into contact and conflict; within cultures, older generations that traditionally passed on survival skills have also become isolated and in new conflict with their progeny.

—While technology adds muscle to our social enterprises, it does not contribute to their guidance. Steering of the disjointed socio-technical system becomes all the more demanding, but the rudder is unwieldy and we lack navigational charts. The implosion of information has not been accompanied by any shared techniques of interpretation.

—The entire decision system appears more highly stretched in terms of resources, exhausted and stressed by adversarial politics and crisis management.

—With growing shocks, disappointments and uncertainty, politicians are baffled; citizens are alienated. Indeed, a paradox arises because people are demanding stronger governmental leadership and intervention to assure attention to evolving public purposes, while at the same time their willingness to pay the tax bill declines, along with their sense of access to and accountability from government.

—As we bump along from crisis to crisis, political leaders focus more intently on short-run issues, neglect balanced consideration of longer term repercussions of present decisions, seek but do not find simple answers.

—In this preoccupation with daily crisis, little energy and inclination remain to examine massive but uncertain threats to survival, and to take pre-crisis preventative measures. Recognition of such social or ecological hazards is often forced to take a back seat to economic imperatives of the present: unemployment, inflation and a compulsive commitment to growth in GNP.

—People are bewildered by this loss in social coherence, accompanied by a loss of confidence in our ability to cope. Social satisfaction as reflected in how people feel about the future may not be significantly greater in technological societies replete with material abundance than in developing nations.

—At the same time, potentially lethal threats multiply and response virtuosity languishes. Instincts of self-preservation seem to be pathologically drained. So we survive by the skin of our teeth.

—As philosopher George Steiner put it so eloquently, we no longer experience history as ascendant.(5) There are too many cardinal points where our lives are threatened, more prone to arbitrary servitude and potential extermination. Yet, in the decay of religious dogma on perfectibility of humankind or a metaphoric imperative of progress, we shall have to deal with our future.

These are the bare bones of the precarious situation inaugurating the 21st century.

Social analysts, who seem in widespread agreement on the symptoms just enumerated, frequently identify one underlying cause—social evolution stuttering because of some sort of limits. But here consensus fades. Some assert limits to growth, to the planet's food production capacity, to available natural resources including energy, to the pollution acceptance of the physical environment. These are the limits to nature. Other writers refer to limits of human nature, the human spirit. Still others, such as H. G. Wells in his essay on "The Mind at the End of its Tether", contend that we have exhausted the intellectual limits of human understanding, even of processing exponentially increasing knowledge. And amidst complexity and the pace of adapting to seductive technology, a fourth set of diagnosticians asserts limits to the functioning of social organization.[6] But with all the storm warnings aflutter, we are still not sure of what is happening. Indeed, as Daniel Bell remarked with singular restraint: "Unhappy is the society that has run out of words to describe what is going on."[7]

What we cannot comprehend, we have little hope of controlling. Yet control over our destiny is a basic tenet of our Western culture. Our first task is to try to understand the situation. To do this we approach by another route: the political limits in steering technology.

The Politicizing of Knowledge: Integrating Technology, Society and the State

This melancholy portrayal of a global predicament, tragic in unfulfilled expectations, is clearly dominated by two notions: the role of technology and the role of national governments. Technology has a great deal to do with the present; it is sure to be at least as significant in the future. It may even influence how we think about the problem. Throughout this book, incidentally, technology is defined as more than technique; rather, as with Webster, "it represents the *totality* of (specialized) means employed to provide objects (or services) necessary for human sustenance and comfort."

Many social philosophers extract technology from the web of human enterprise to proclaim it either villain or savior. In the latter camp are those who believe planetary social needs and wants can be met by catering to more or better technological initiatives, the "technological fix." Others are profoundly convinced that technology is a new social disease, so virulent that the only route to congeniality and sanity is to turn it off.

While as opposite as Cain and Abel, these twin propositions are children of the same basic notion that for three decades has been the opening gambit to this entire issue: science and technology have a profound and ubiquitous impact on society. Given both its benign and its adverse effects, technology has been blithely assumed as subject to both taming and tuning to fulfill human purposes. Now we are not so confident.

In what follows we fasten on the opposite side of the society–technology dyad—that the more important issue is the impact that society has on technology. In other words, it is not only that specialized scientific knowledge and engineering application govern whether technology produces socially satisfactory outcomes. Rather, it is that the cultural backdrop of our society, the structure and the procession of human affairs, have the most critical influence on the applications of technology—on the goals to which it is directed, the resources invested in research, development and implementation strategies and, most important, on selection of beneficiaries. These are the overarching decisions. In contemporary societies—capitalist, socialist, developing—such choices are largely those of the state; that is, of national governments.

This emphasis on the contemporary role of governments is widely accepted across the full ideological spectrum, from rugged individualists who complain of its burden to those who have lost confidence in the marketplace as the major device for social decision making. The bald fact is that in Western democracies, government expenditures approximate one-third of their GNP, including a substantial fraction for military technology. By functioning as a spender, government exerts enormous leverage in maintaining the market. By its monetary policies, government manipulates it to the point of suspending or superseding free market processes. By other policies, it stimulates and regulates private technological enterprise to the point that public–private boundaries are blurred. Yet, as Galbraith vigorously contends, public instruments for private purposes have public consequences.[(8)]

The role of government and the role of technology have grown together, and it will be argued in some detail later that each has grown because of the other. The key notion here, however, is that it is government far more than the marketplace that defines the rules which structure overall social behavior, including that involved with the steering of technology.

In short, the modern state defines the political space in which the key technological acts occur. Government is thus becoming more technological and technology more political.

The resulting politicizing of knowledge is nowhere better defined than in the funding of research and development. Governmental sponsorship predominates. As exemplified by the energy dilemma, more choices have to be made on support for solar, geothermal, wind, ocean, biomass and coal research as alternatives to nuclear fission, and these decisions are conspicuously sited in the political arena. The same holds true for choices of weapons development.

To explain the society–technology–government interaction another way, technology can be thought of as an amplifier. By lever and wheel, then the steam engine, technology became an amplifier of human muscle. By the computer it became an amplifier of the human mind. Now we discover technology as an amplifier of social appetites, of social conflict and stress, of governmental dominance and of defects in our social institutions, including government.

This inversion—this looking at things in terms of social influences on technology—is not merely a neat semantic trick. From the earlier catechism, several unsettling clues of possible technological malfunctioning emerged other than the narrower ingredients of its internal dynamics. These include cognitive dissonance, institutional misbehavior and impotent policy making.

It should be emphasized that technology is a means, seldom an end in itself. Thus the overarching goals in employing technology are to obtain socially desirable outcomes in both the present and the future. This clearly means intervention to prevent alarming trends from becoming destiny.

Far more is then involved than just speeding up or slowing down the generators of technology. We are confronted with the herculean task of finding those cardinal points and directions where institutional, social and individual behavior might be altered.

Although this second formulation of the impact of social process on technology may be the key to understanding, it opens a Pandora's box of discouraging portent. If we accept that notion of behavior change literally, the challenge to scholarship is staggering. For one thing, the breadth of inquiry must encompass all of the social apparatus that deals with technology, the entire anatomy of civilization. With that wide-angled lens, far more is involved than the research and development activities that too often have been mistakenly equated to technology. That analysis requires probing the lattice of social, technical, economic, legal, political and institutional processes by which technology is directed to needs and wants. In the United States, for example, the scope extends from grass-roots culture and tradition to decision making in the White House and the Congress. And the task requires qualitative measures of social performance, tools for diagnosis and theories of social change, which neither are readily available nor have been proved credible in application.

To keep the primary arguments of the book within bounds, some limits must be set arbitrarily:

—This approach to the future is developed within the context of Western culture and democratic government. By no means does this boundary exclude the rest of the world; indeed, planetary scales of peril and transnational interconnections are dealt with explicitly.

—Heavy emphasis is placed on the role of public policy as a critical ingredient of survival because it constitutes the primary guidance signals by which the separate institutions of our society steer individually toward collective goals, and because implementation of policy generates many, and perhaps the most salient, consequences for the years ahead.

—While it is recognized that steering must be accomplished by an enormous number of topically distinct policies, none of these is examined in detail. Instead, the analysis focuses on the overriding processes by which policy is generated, evaluated, implemented and modified.

Because of the time which must elapse between political goal setting and the implementation of a program (time devoted to debate, compromise, and resource allocation) policy serves as the bridge between present and future. Thus, in looking to the future, we examine the predictive behavior of policy makers and of key institutions in terms of two modes of political decision: those made and questioned, and those neglected or deliberately avoided. These can also be phrased in terms of our earlier two questions: What will happen, if . . .? And, what may happen, unless . . .?[9]

Given that technology is called upon to produce certain explicit benefits, and given surprises and unwanted future consequences, the choices to be considered are in terms not of what *can* we do, but of what *ought* we do. Should technological initiatives be undertaken *without* imaginative inquiry into possible consequences, or should technologically induced change be anticipated by pre-crisis impact assessment and, to use military parlance, protective reaction?

Because technology, its artifacts and forces of social change have such powerful influences on the future, any failure to speculate on and to gauge impacts of the decision, and to monitor impacts subsequently, becomes a sin of commission.

Equally vital are the corresponding delinquencies of omission: indifference to the omens of massive but uncertain calamity that are neglected, undervalued, or treated at random, and the inadequate pursuit of promising technical options.

At this stage in human history, an enormous range of alternative futures is possible. Their diversity is at least as great as the spectrum of cultures, value preferences and levels of material well-being currently found on the planet. And, judging by science fiction fantasies of genetic manipulation, there could even be races of men and women different from present inhabitants. These possibilities could be classified. Then, with some scale of desirable options, one definition of Utopia could be adopted as a goal.

Survival: A Neglected Governmental Responsibility

Instead of searching more stubbornly for paradise, polling, delineating and distilling what people want, a different approach is explored. We pose the obverse in terms of what people do *not* want. In other words, we deal with the future in terms of potential threats to survival over a wide range of risks. Then, in the context of social decision making, we inquire as to the salient role, responsibility, disposition and capability in government, present or needed, for avoiding calamity.

For brevity as well as for structure of research, this inquiry is translated to a fundamental hypothesis in the form of one salient question: Why does the policy apparatus act as though it were deaf to signals about the future?

Implicit in this question is a set of premises that deserves to be made explicit.

First, the central mood of the social decision process favors the short rather than the longer run; or, put in economic jargon, the system heavily discounts the future. Second, there is the implication that, notwithstanding the high noise level, certain signals of approaching danger are present, credible, readable and subject to prophylactic action.

It follows then that listening and acting can make a difference; indeed, all the difference. That is to say, human evolution has reached a critical stage where neglect of future consequences could entail a penalty for decision error so economically expensive, so politically strenuous, so environmentally disastrous or so inimical to the human spirit that certain trade-offs by deferring short term gratification are deemed worthwhile whatever the immediate cost or inconvenience.

At a time when both capitalist and socialist governments have translated the prevailing ethos into social welfare for the individual, the historic role of public institutions has been sidetracked—that of ensuring survival of the species. To be sure, in the name of national security, the arms race continues. Technology has become a prime agent of foreign policy for survival of individual nations. But the broader question of transcendental threats remains.

A refocusing of governmental responsibilities may thus be urgent. This is consistent with orthodox views on the role of government: to make the most fundamental decisions, to make them effectively, to dramatize issues and focus the political energies of society on the choices ahead.

By no means does fastening attention on survival diminish the importance of the obverse issue—the goals and utopian images of social progress. There is already abundant, even breathless, literature on that question. At this time, however, the world may be entering an unstable phase of history wherein attention to disaster avoidance is a necessary if not sufficient condition to have a future at all.

People may be an endangered species.

In such logic there is a presumption that people care about the future. There is also a presumption of rationality in thoughtful, deliberate action to assure continuity of the human race. On the basis of how people act rather than what they say, the evidence is shaky as to whether either premise is universally true.

As to embracing the future as though it mattered, there is a steady drumbeat in our culture for instant gratification, aided and abetted by the technological embrace. In this preoccupation with "me, now," it is not necessary to speculate about philosophical dedication to generations yet unborn. The time scale of our concern extends no further ahead than the lifetime of people on earth today. We thus are dealing with long term self-interest and associated trade-offs versus an undisguised cultural propensity for immediate satisfaction.

The question of rationality is somewhat more slippery. For one thing, the notion of rationality cannot be dealt with in the abstract.

We must ask, rationality for whom? If here we discover a diversity and conflict of self-interest among different parties, then each may be motivated by what is rational for him, even if it appears irrational or at least nonrational to others. This is to some extent a cop-out because it begs the question of altruism in relation to the future. To avoid the quagmire of speculation on basic tenets of human behavior, it is worth recalling that altruism has been a staple of Christian ethics for 2000 years. In secular terms, altruism is very often a manifestation of long term self-interest, rather than compassion, and if the sociobiologists are correct, perhaps even a matter of long term genetic evolution as a trait that tends to preserve the species.

In our culture, people seem embarrassed to talk about compassion and love. Yet, these qualities play such a key role in the human condition that they must ultimately be acknowledged even in the cold, impersonal theatre of public policy.

Thus, these sometimes paradoxical dimensions of human nature—self-interest and love—cannot be disposed of by arbitrary definitions or assumptions, because any examination of the future is based on a premise that survival of humankind is not simply a biological matter of preserving a physically endangered species. That the individual represents so much more is reflected in culture and even in law. In addition to its concern for life asserted by the United States Declaration of Independence, there is equal dedication to liberty and to the pursuit of happiness.

Other democracies can lay claim to the same basic goals and similar charters for their government. These represent a minority of all the sovereign nations and a small fraction of world population. But for this moment in history they collectively represent a major economic and political power, reinforced by the energy of the ideals to which they are committed. Yet their way of life is threatened. Thus, the notion emerges that survival of the species, defined as significantly more than biological, is a special responsibility of those governments whose fundamental precepts are at stake.

CHAPTER 2

Threats to Survival

An Inventory of Global Dangers: From Nuclear Terror to Loss of Freedom

Humankind has forever lived at risk. For primal man there was almost always the threat of hunger and of pestilence. There was also risk of bodily harm from accident, from encounter with wild animals, from natural disaster and extremes of weather, and from violence at the hands of other individuals. Quite apart from physical dangers has been the peril of brutality through psychological–emotional threats—of deprivation of basic human rights, freedom and dignity, deprivation of equitable access to resources, and deprivation of individual opportunity for equanimity and self-expression. It is an irony of civilization that at any time only a very small fraction of the world's population ever lived securely with reduced risks. A small elite has frequently organized the clan and community; exploited, even enslaved the majority. A spectre if not the reality of doom has been continuous and widespread, periodically taking more solid and somber form.[10]

Things were recently getting better. The statistics on longevity confirm marked advances in public health over the past three centuries, but in the West progress seems to have reached a plateau. Western democracies for two hundred years have provided a framework for human self-expression that, although not spreading rapidly today, has become something of a model and source of hope to those whose spirits yearn for freedom and know it is at least possible.

In the past 30 years, however, the phenomenon of risk has changed. Given newspaper headlines that include, incidentally, reference to the selected inventory of global dangers discussed here, one wonders whether the situation in the 20th century shows progress beyond the greater control of wild animals and disease!

Because contemporary perils have been nominated by so many credible analysts and dramatized by familiar experience, no strenuous inquiry has been undertaken to generate additional images of Hell. These conspicuous dangers are briefly outlined in the following discussion. Some few are elaborated. Then all are evaluated in terms of the scale of threat and indices of prevention. Finally, we examine a qualitative difference that seems to emerge in this contemporary phalanx of dangers as compared to the past.

The danger of nuclear warfare[11]

This enormity in terms of deaths, radioactive poisoning, social and physical destruction was first discussed publicly by atomic scientists in the late 1940s. Various scenarios of destruction were generated as images of the future, almost all based on accidental or deliberate nuclear exchange between the East–West superpowers and their allies. That sensitive balance remains, albeit now burdened by change, both in quality and in quantity of warheads (via MIRV, for example). But the situation is growing swiftly more precarious. More nations such as India, Israel, Brazil, South Africa, Pakistan, West Germany, have reached nuclear maturity with access to weapons-grade plutonium, some surreptitiously through misuse of nuclear research or power facilities. Added to that risk of proliferation is the possibility of nuclear materials and weapons potential being purchased on a black market, or obtained illegally by irresponsible leaders in otherwise nonnuclear countries, or by terrorist groups intent on nuclear blackmail.

The danger of widespread famine and resulting disorder[12]

The Malthusian disparity between a rapidly growing world population and available food, while an ancient peril, now attains new scales of human suffering, with global rather than local and isolated repercussions. One-third of the world's population is continuously undernourished. Populations in Indonesia, the Philippines and Latin America burgeon with scientific advances of death control through public health measures not accompanied by advances in birth control.

On the other side of the equation, technological progress in enhanced food production has been accompanied by vulnerability of monoculture to pests, disease and drought, by weak food distribution infrastructure, by miniscule international reserves, by limits to yet uncultivated agricultural land and fresh water, and by higher costs of energy and fertilizer. Not only does the mismatch of food and population continue on a planetary scale, the imbalance grows between the rich, well-fed nations and the others. Indeed, poor nations intent on enhancing foreign exchange have exported one-third more in tonnage over the past three decades of protein rich foods, such as soybeans, seed oil and fish meal, but with an increase in value of less than 5%. So they never catch up. Meanwhile, the few producers of food surpluses may be reaching limits of sustainable harvests, possibly exhausting land, depleting underground aquifers and yielding rich farm lands to urban encroachment. And marine sources of protein suffer from overfishing. As starvation more continuously reaches larger numbers of people, internal political stability will be jeopardized and violence is predictable. Externally, as deprived nations make nonnegotiable demands on the affluent, in a world made conscious of such tribulations by both TV and diplomatic networks, the previously limited boundaries of disaster could politically envelop everyone.

The danger of global environmental poisoning[13]

At stake here is the interruption or modification of natural processes on a planetary scale and in such a fashion as to be inimical to health of all forms of life. These problems of global pollution were stressed at the 1972 United Nations Conference on the Human Environment and are currently under study by the UN Environmental Program.

An example of such a threat is continued nuclear testing and its potential of loading the atmosphere and ocean with slowly decaying radioactive compounds that could induce harmful effects of the sort visited on Japanese fishermen inadvertently downwind from nuclear tests in the Pacific. Even more catastrophic would be worldwide genetic damage to those unborn. Fortunately, prophylactic measures were instituted to head off such a calamity, an intervention discussed later in terms of a rehearsal for disaster. But other hazards of this type could arise from accidental release of high level, long-lived radioisotopes from waste disposal dumps that at this date are still a topic of active study and debate.

The ubiquitous presence of DDT in upper layers of the ocean could alter marine biological processes and thus either destroy the food chain or render seafood inedible. Agricultural pesticides entering the world ecosystem exceed one million tons a year with unknown effects. Continued use of freon (chlorofluorocarbons) in aerosols could reduce the capacity of the upper atmosphere to filter out ultraviolet radiation and increase risks of skin cancer. Quite apart from the question of global poisoning is the risk of inadvertent climate modification, discussed separately.

The portents of danger from global environmental poisoning may best be visualized from innumerable and well-documented lethal events of a more localized nature.

The danger of large-scale local environmental poisoning[14]

While individual, localized insults to the environment may not appear to warrant inclusion in this inventory, the number and frequency of incidents suggest they do. Examples of this threat abound. Forty-four Japanese died of mercury poisoning from eating fish contaminated with industrial waste. Many more were permanently crippled. In Hopewell, Virginia, Kepone waste from pesticide manufacture incapacitated industrial workers in the plant and leaked into local sewage disposal systems, then into the James River and the Chesapeake Bay before detection, rendering fish products from a wide area inedible. Similar experiences occurred with PCB in Lake Ontario, the Hudson and Connecticut rivers; dieldrin induced fish kills in the Mississippi. Slaughtering was mandated of beef cattle in Michigan accidentally poisoned by pesticides in their food; New York residents were moved from homes unwittingly built on dumps of dangerous chemicals; the hazard was announced in 1976 of potential poisoning in the Mediterranean from 300 tons of tetraethyl lead aboard the ship *Cavtat* sunk near the Italian coast. Massive oil spills from tanker wrecks regularly hit the headlines. Chemical plant explosions in Italy required large-scale belated evacuation pending massive decontamination. Radionuclides from various nuclear processes have been dumped indiscriminately in the ocean, as have heavy metals and other industrial wastes, although now subject to more control in the United States and a few other nations. Rail and truck accidents highlight the vast quantity and variety of hazardous materials on the move and the range of hazards involved.

The total effects here may not be known for a generation, but epidemiologists already suspect that toxic substances in the environment are a major source of cancer. All of which led the U.S. Council on Environmental Quality to conclude in 1974 that the development of environmental indices was in "an unsatisfactory state."

Dangers of inadvertent climate modification(15)

Variations in weather from year to year are well known, if inconvenient. Nevertheless, for some decades scientists have recognized that increasing loads on the atmosphere of carbon dioxide, particulates and heat from burning fossil fuels could upset the climate. That is, the long term average weather over huge areas might be significantly altered. However, the complexity of the atmospheric system so defies analysis that it is uncertain whether the net result would be a greenhouse effect, so heating the earth as to melt the ice cap, raise ocean levels, and flood all coastal cities, or whether the opposite effect would prevail, chilling the earth into a new ice age. Indeed, the added heat from *all* types of energy consumption may prove a hazard as the total zooms exponentially.

At lesser geophysical scales, but no less serious to human activity, could be disruption of major rainfall patterns from human intervention, critically altering food production and supplies of fresh water for all purposes. The growth of desert regions in biblical times probably resulted from human misuse of the natural grasslands. Now, wholesale depletion of tropical forests progresses at a fast pace; oil films form on large patches of the ocean; high-flying aircraft disrupt the stratosphere and add cloud cover. Lacking wise preventive measures, all pose potentially irreversible disruptions of natural climate.

Dangers of urban deterioration, social and economic chaos[16]

The cliché of "urban crisis" represents a thicket of separate but interrelated phenomena, manifested worldwide. First, not only are populations growing everywhere; they more and more tend to concentrate in cities. Sao Paulo, Brazil, for example, which numbered two million in 1950 and eight million in 1970, is projected to top 20 million by the year 2000. But jobs and housing do not match the immigration. Whatever the social and economic forces at work, building a megalopolis depends on familiar technologies of structures, water supply, sewage disposal and transportation. The problem is that as cities expand, an almost universal experience has been loss of a sense of community, indeed in both the quality of environment and the quality of life. Then residents flash symptoms of stress and alienation.

In the United States a different set of problems attends the aging of cities where populations remain static but change their composition. Encouraged by federal tax breaks on home mortgages and a cultural set toward single family dwellings in suburbia, the middle class moves out, leaving the old, the young, the poor and the less educated. Both the job market and tax base decline, and demand increases for social services. Widespread violence and fear of violence in American cities reached incandescence literally in the late 1960s and still smoulders. Fundamental municipal services have been interrupted by strikes. Bankruptcy and unemployment threaten as the manufacturing and commercial base seeks more congenial environments, and political power shifts from coalitions of ethnic and private economic groups to municipal labor unions with insatiable demands. Vulnerability sharpens to technical collapse with catastrophic traffic jams, mass transit struggling to meet all costs out of the fare box, electrical blackouts (in New York), water stoppages (Montgomery County, Maryland), bridge accidents (Chesapeake Bay).

Dangers of resource depletion[17]

Whatever the aspirations of the disadvantaged majority on the planet and the desire to assist by the blessed minority, it is a rude fact of life that the material standard of living enjoyed by a few Western nations and Japan will never be in the cards for everyone. There simply is a limit to availability of nonrenewable natural resources at acceptable costs. As to solid minerals, richness of ore deposits declines and costs of exploration grow. Recycling of scrap iron continues to be neglected.

As to energy, the per capita consumption by 215 million Americans is almost ten times the world average. Extrapolation to 4 billion people alive today is unthinkable. Clearly this disparity exposes a vital moral issue. The universal dependence on petroleum was all too clearly demonstrated by the 1973 OPEC moratorium and the resultant sharp increases in price. On an international scale, a pattern of dependency, interdependency and uncertainty emerged. On the domestic front, the response was controversy, vacillation and unwillingness to introduce new measures to conserve resources. Only the multinational oil companies and the OPEC nations appear to be better off. Classical market processes of supply and demand do not work. And, according to the most recent authoritative study, a looming crossover of world supply and demand for petroleum threatens a near term political crisis.

Even renewable resources are being exploited so relentlessly as to threaten future availability. Statistics on fresh water, forests and fishery stocks demonstrate man's failure to apply principles of conservation. Like nonrenewable resources, the renewable base undergoes depletion.

History teaches us that with scarcity comes aggression.

Dangers of global disorder from increasing economic disparity among nations[(18)]

The prospects of intramural chaos engendered by urban problems has a larger scale counterpart of international disorder triggered by the fact that the rich nations are becoming richer and, at least relatively, the poor poorer. So pronounced and worrisome is this trend that it has led to rhetoric if not remedial action of "the new economic order." By no means have the advanced nations been unmindful of this trend and its portents of danger made worse by sharp increases in energy costs, but only a few have responded with compassion and altruism to share even a smidgen of their wealth. The dramatic growth of OPEC surpluses from the West has only inflamed the problem. Notwithstanding massive programs of foreign aid, doses of loans from international banks and the mystique of technology transfer, the basic pattern remains unbroken. Poverty within and terrorism without add to the level of global tension. And the approaching threshold of economic collapse of some developing countries could spill over to the wealthy nations as massive, unsecured loans are defaulted. Officials of the Carter Administration have stated that these international economic problems far overshadow political issues.

Dangers of system failures—institutional and policy malfunctioning[19]

The point will shortly be made that technological progress has been an instrinsic ingredient of civilization, and that change to improve prospects of individual survival simultaneously involves both technical and social innovation. Public and private institutions and their steering by policy decisions have evolved as an essential mechanism to employ or deploy technological advances in transportation, communication, education, housing, resource development, criminal justice, public health, public works and social services. Today, however, no one feels satisfied with their performance. The problem reaches new heights of concern when one or another of these instrumentalities seems in danger of collapse. In America, which has led the world in both technical progress and social reform, that prospect seems imminent in several situations, most clearly in health care delivery. The twin commitments to universality of services and to high quality based on technical artifacts have escalated costs to the point of economic exhaustion. Few if any restraints such as competition exist to keep costs low and quality high. The life styles of the medical profession, coupled with threats of suit for malpractice, force application of high-priced diagnostic tests as the routine basis of medical performance that should instead be employed far more sparingly. And fraud in Medicare is documented nationwide. Simply broadening insurance coverage without fundamental changes can only accelerate the collapse, changes in attitudes towards preventive medicine, towards health education and towards rebalancing priorities in medical research.

Other systems that we Americans depend on in a technological culture reveal similar, if yet uncrystallized, signs of dysfunction or actual breakdown: the railroads; housing for the young, old and poor; technology that is marked by sharply increased quantity and ubiquity of information but without public understanding; systems of regulation that may inadvertently strangle innovation; and educational systems not geared to future social needs.

Such prospects in technological underperformance are so manifest that the National Academy of Engineering, when responding to a government request for nominations of urgent technical research applicable to national needs, concluded that first priority should be given to studies of institutional malfunctioning. For, they said, without correctives in this arena, the potential of science and engineering to produce socially satisfactory outcomes would be frustrated.

Dangers of loss in freedom[20]

As these systems sputter everywhere on the globe, as urban environments deteriorate, resources are depleted and subject to vicious competition, and as the new economic order is retarded, the tendency increases everywhere to inject correctives by stronger political controls. Pernicious concentration of political power follows, through stages of constraints on freedom, of oppressive coercion, and even of enslavement. The problem of incipient tyranny goes beyond malevolent intent. Those merely with ambitions for social control now have available a whole new array of technological tools: electronic techniques for eavesdropping, for access to privileged data in computer banks, for subliminal propaganda in the media, and for either psychological or physical intimidation.

To be sure, the cultural ideal of human rights as viewed in the West is not universal, although we presume that the desire to be free as well as to be alive is a fundamental quality of the human spirit. It is, nevertheless, a fact of life that freedom is never absolute and, even relative to contemporary Western mores of freedom of speech, of political choice and of individual opportunity, it is found among only a small fraction of the world's peoples. The U.S. State Department has reported that most of the 82 countries receiving foreign aid are violating these rights.

But even in democracies, "friendly fascism" is threatened. The dramatic, albeit temporary, withdrawal of freedom in India in 1974 is a case in point. To achieve their goals, national leaders may be tempted to crush dissent, and, as discussed later, the United States has had more than one close shave. In wartime, many dimensions of freedom are willingly sacrificed. If the present situation reaches high enough levels of stress, people may voluntarily trade freedom for promises of material rewards or for public order. No one can feel confident that commitments to human rights are permanent.

Dangers of pathological shifts in values[21]

The exercise of political power may extend well beyond withdrawal of human rights. Within memory is the extermination by the Nazis of 6 million Jews. What is so astonishing is that a society considered technically advanced, culturally enriched and, by modern standards, civilized could condone such a holocaust. Mass murder was the political solution to Adolf Hitler's imagined problems. There is an uneasy suspicion of history repeating itself in Uganda and Iraq and, with the disappearance of hundreds of thousands of citizens, in Cambodia.

The seemingly remote and abstract threat of a pathological shift in values became harsh reality in November 1978 with the obscene horror of mass suicide at Jonestown, Guyana. While everyone now broods over the cause of such a calamity, the fact of its occurrence serves as a graphic reminder of what can happen *today* to large numbers of people.

Other manifestations of a pathological culture include pressures for citizens to act as informers on neighbors or family, and generally to excise nonconformity in life styles and points of view. We are already concerned about whether a constant TV diet of violence fundamentally weakens compassion.

At different scales, political murder and torture continue in dozens of countries today, well documented by Amnesty International and with full knowledge of the citizenry.

One new twist on a pathological shift in values may be opened up by genetic engineering. Here, specific molecules of DNA are spliced onto carrier genes and introduced into a host cell which, in turn, incorporates the new gene itself. New organisms result, potentially as boundless and unpredictable as life itself. There is currently a hot debate on potential health hazards from a laboratory accident. But one possibility so opened up would be genetic manipulation to produce new forms of human life, perhaps under direction and to meet purposes of political authority.

The question that lurks over the horizon and ignites the same type of nightmares as nuclear conflict is whether any nation under the superposition of threats just enumerated would not acquiesce to a pathological shift in values as the price for imagined physical survival.

Common characteristics of emerging threats

This inventory of dangers clearly represents a subjective choice by the author and is intended to be illustrative rather than comprehensive. It is of interest, nevertheless, to compare the critical issues set forth here with a comparable list compiled in September 1978 by the Congressional Office of Technology Assessment. Its objective was to formulate a set of priorities for future studies that would be distinguished by their fundamental contribution to long-term national policies, rather than, as discussed later, as subjects of current legislation. To develop their list, OTA undertook a nationwide poll, followed by a synthesis to a master list that met criteria of national relevance based on estimated severity of social or economic impact.

Some thirty-two topics met the test. Of these, twenty-five fall within ten of the eleven previously mentioned categories of long-term hazard. The eleventh category, not explicitly covered in OTA's program, concerns threats to freedom. The remaining seven OTA topics not represented here are defined by explicit technologies rather than by social dilemmas, an alternative mode of impact analysis. The selected topics include computers, broadband electronic telecommunications, transportation, including newer versions of an SST, prescription drugs, utilization of extraterrestrial space and various health technologies. The timetable for completion of OTA studies, incidentally, requires conducting about ten in parallel, with initial reports available in 1980.

In the interest of brevity, details of these critical issues have been left to readers to pursue in the referenced literature, for each could justify booklength explanation. One example of nuclear warfare is chosen for subsequent elaboration because of its clear credibility as a massive threat. First, however, it may be instructive to examine common properties of these hazards.

Virtually all involve technology; are subject to human ignition, deliberately or inadvertently; entail hazards potentially affecting far greater numbers of people than ever before, many as innocent victims. Not only is the scale geographically extended laterally. The risks also become a longitudinally projected endowment for progeny, for technological progress has not automatically fostered a ***noblesse oblige*** of each generation to leave the world a better place to live in.

Other features of this new class of risk are their novelty and speed of injection. Indeed, there is an abrupt discontinuity in the nature of threats manifest in just 30 years; clearly they outspace alacrity of response. Moreover, interactions among the threats and the complexities of social organization make it substantially more difficult to respond.

In practically every case, the government has been alerted, but our sense of reality tells us that measures of intervention have been weak and ineffective, sometimes counterproductive. At the same time, the public is lulled to nonchalance on grounds that alarms are exaggerated, that progress is being made, that other, more immediate issues require priority, and that having survived through a continuous exposure to peril, we shall ultimately find some solution. Hazards may or may not be worse for the individual than what has gone before, and that speculation may not even be relevant. But they pose a different challenge to the human species as a whole.

The Nuclear Example

For the skeptic, some amplification of just one example may be instructive.

First on any list is the threat of nuclear warfare. The explosive power of such weapons and their low cost, the speed and accuracy of delivery, the relative ease of surprise attack and their range, completely alter the nature of warfare. It is now of global rather than of local dimensions.

The suffering of survivors and possible genetic damage to children of survivors confer on this military invention a scale of horror and devastation that is almost beyond human comprehension. Indeed, the threat is so anonymous and invisible, except in taxes for national security, and the consequences are so calamitous, as to be dismissed from the daily concerns of almost everyone. Because individuals feel powerless to cope with it, responsibility for survival automatically passes to our political leadership. And that responsibility is all the more sobering because there is no absolute technical defense at any price. As Kenneth Boulding has said,[(22)] "unconditional viability has disappeared." And so we live at the mercy of a few powerful men.

The gravity of this situation is heightened because of two factors. First, peace, or at least the inhibition of nuclear exchange, depends on a mutual credibility of threat. This interconnectedness entails information about each other's technical prowess, national intentions and character. Secondly, action depends on a handful of leaders whose individual stability, response to stress and images of reality control the action.

A problem which was already critical when only two superpowers possessed the bomb has been incalculably escalated by its spread to more nations. Nuclear blackmail becomes a possibility at the hands of terrorists or emotionally disturbed national leaders.

Clearly, this scale and mode of risk is intolerable. Either we learn to manage conflict by other means, or, as John Platt asserts,[(23)] we shall be annihilated. All responsible national leaders perceive this menace, and for two decades de-escalation of openly tabulated nuclear weaponry has been pursued earnestly through the 30-nation Committee on Disarmament of the UN. It was the theme of the UN Special Assembly on Disarmament in 1978. Yet the number of warheads has not diminished.

Far more uncertain, but potentially as devastating, is the emergence of an outlaw culture. The world frequently has had to deal with this problem on a smaller scale with airplane hijacking and political kidnapping, and not without fatalities. Now, a new blackmail weapon is emerging. Notwithstanding President Jimmy Carter's attempt to limit nuclear power plants, sales continue worldwide. Each opens possibilities of theft. The errors in accounting procedures for nuclear materials, the vulnerability of unguarded facilities, the expected growth in traffic of plutonium for reprocessing, all widen opportunities for mischief. So we have a race between disaster and risk reduction.

Cautions about this latent menace have been publicized, with convincing scenarios—for example, by Taylor and Willrich.[24] In May 1977 the alarm bells rang with two new realities. The U.S. Government Accounting Office reported for the second time to the Congress that several thousand pounds of weapons-grade uranium had been mislaid over the years in commercial nuclear plants, enough to make dozens of nuclear bombs. While there was no claim that it had been stolen, the apparently careless accounting procedures made it impossible to say with complete certainty what had happened to the missing material. Knowledge of these discrepancies in nuclear inventories had been carefully concealed.

The second possible diversion to military or terrorist groups for weapons development arose with the announcement in 1977 by the European Economic Community that 200 tons of uranium ore had mysteriously disappeared nine years before and that the loss had also been concealed in a gigantic cover-up. The material, shipped under a commercial trade name of PLUMBAT, vanished after leaving Antwerp in a small freighter destined for Morocco but diverted, on paper, to Milan. It never arrived. Apparently, the International Atomic Energy Authority that was created as a watchdog for potentially illegal activities felt it lacked authority to investigate; belated inquiries by security services of Italy, Belgium, West Germany and the United States CIA are said to have led to dead ends. Yet, the sale and resale of the transporting ship, sabotage of its log and shuffling of bills of lading clearly reveal a clever plot. Given that the ore could be processed into 30 bombs of the size dropped on Japan, the conservative London *Times* on May 8, 1977, felt obliged to label the account "how to hijack a holocaust."

To complete this picture, in October 1978, the FBI charged three men in the U.S. with conspiracy to attempt hijacking of a naval submarine carrying torpedos with nuclear warheads.

Scales of Lethality

The full significance of this inventory of perils is easier to

TABLE 1. *Ranking of perils*

Menace	Worst case casualties or seriously affected people (millions)	Worst case imminence (years)	Probabilities and trends of peril	Pre-crisis intervention		
				Minimum time required (years)	Probability of successful technical–economic intervention (scale 1–10) (low to high probability)	Probability of successful political intervention (scale 1–10)
Nuclear war	2000	0	Moderate, increasing	10	8	2
Hunger, famine and world disorder	1000	10	High, increasing	15	8	5
Global environmental poisoning	2000	35	Low, increasing	20	8	7
Large-scale local environmental poisoning	500	10	High, increasing	10	9	7
Inadvertent climate modification	1500	75	Low, increasing	50	3	7
Urban bankruptcy and chaos	500	15	High, increasing	30	5	3
Resource depletion	1500	30	High, increasing	20	7	4
Economic collapse	1000	15	Medium, increasing	15	6	5
Institutional collapse	500	15	Medium, increasing	25	5	5
Loss of freedoms	700	20	Medium, stable	10	–	4
Pathological shifts in values	3000	30	Medium, increasing	30	–	3

comprehend when tabulated along lines suggested by John Platt and analyzed as to scale of menace in terms of projected casualties and of imminence, time required for pre-crisis intervention, feasibility of technical intervention and ease of political intervention (Table 1).[25]

Although a vast simplification and, frankly, a subjective judgment, this table projects in stark terms the vital dimensions of the problem. First, all of the projected risks potentially affect large numbers of people; many are lethal. Second, all have a time horizon of 75 years or less, within limits of life for those already born; nuclear war, with a worst-case imminence of zero, could be triggered anytime. Third, probabilities of occurrence, while ranging from estimates of low to high, are all increasing or at best stable. Next, in some cases the time for successful intervention is longer than the worst-case imminence, thus signaling for priority attention. Finally, political feasibility of hazard reduction is generally estimated as less than the techno-economic feasibility.

Considering that perils are evolving in tandem, not in series, these prophetic omens of the future set the stage for action. All involve such grave consequences that, even before risks are understood precisely, extreme caution is the only prudent course.

Yet society does not seem to be equipping itself to survive. Our social energies and investments in risk abatement do not accord with the levels of risk. Far more attention seems given in the press, legislative debate and citizen activism to a moratorium in hunting whales than to arms control.

Such indifference to peril might be cast in the black-humor commentary of the fellow who, having fallen off the top of the Empire State Building, remarked in passing the fiftieth floor, "Everything's OK so far."

This allegory suggests a strategic point: the salient challenge is *prevention of disaster*, and at that, prevention by political means, a constant theme in what follows.

Clearly the way ahead is dangerous. Despite probable limits to human nature, to physical resources and to social policy to reduce risk, we sustain a faith that life can prevail over death; but safely traversing the edge of the precipice will surely require new social learning about survival, and soon.

Coping with Risk: Safety and Self-preservation

While life experience tells us that survival entails both determination and skill, most individuals do not approach this question self-consciously or systematically. Yet it is important to comprehend those mechanisms that afford self-preservation. As we shall see, these also apply to questions of survival of the clan.

By fantasies of potential threat, or even rehearsals such as fire drills, an individual develops a repertoire of mental patterns that constitute tests of early warning signals. When patterns representing threats are perceived and recognized, the individual responds either by panic, by evasive maneuver or retreat, by aggression, by prevention without loss in self-esteem, or by problem-solving countermeasures. Our major focus on this threat–response sequence and associated social behavior will be on the latter two strategies.

To elaborate, early warning perceptions of hazard may be classified as (1) human instinct for safety and self-preservation, (2) indoctrination by family and community, (3) environmental cautions based on education or personal experience of a routine nature (such as awareness of poisons), (4) subtle changes in the state of the perceived environment that arouse suspicion, vigilance and sensitivity to or search for additional information, (5) explicit alarms of danger. These five modes of alerting represent increasing levels of consciousness that range from deeply subconscious premonition to full concentration of sensory attention. All reinforce preparedness of the individual to deal with the emergency.

This quest for safety, incidentally, is a social judgment of acceptable risk and not an absolute number derived scientifically.[(26)] How safe is safe is a matter of probabilities and estimates of severity of harm.

Thus, following an alert, our mental processes involve a situation analysis, a safety/risk assessment and a decision. The situation analysis employs both appreciation of the external warning and memory. What is the consistency of association between the perceived threat and its consequences, and how certainly is that cause related to effect? Of what quality are the warning signals as to clarity, freedom from noise or overload, authenticity, familiarity? Can they be interpreted with minimum ambiguity and uncertainty, and in terms of threat patterns;

and if they occur in profusion, can the different threats be separated and ranked in order? As to risk assessment, what alternatives for action are available, at what cost in resources, how soon and with what estimated effectiveness? Can consequences of no action or of weak response be tolerated? Is the response debilitated by lack of preparation, by distraction, confusion, complexity of implementation, inadequate resources or sheer exhaustion? And finally as to a decision to accept risk, what are our criteria for choice?

Lest this description of catastrophe avoidance sound pedantic or structured for application to grand military strategy, consider the practiced, subconscious thoughts and conscious actions taken to drive an auto safely, an experience familiar to everyone.

These involve driver training, familiarization with limits of vehicle performance, such as braking distance of new or rented cars, the strategic role of maps when traversing strange territory. Then there are the tactical demands for good visibility of the road ahead, cautionary alertness on curves, in darkness, rain, snow or fog, defensive driving patterns in heavy traffic with inattentive or alcoholic drivers, driver responsiveness to routine road signs or to temporary warnings of a special nature. Finally, there is the problem arising from poor information at unmarked crossroads, from confusion of multiple signs or unexpected indicators of freeway access.

This analogy should prove useful later when we examine the future in terms of driving—the need for clear visibility through the windshield, and the continuous processing of these visual cues to maintain safe margins between us and the vehicle ahead or the edge of the road, and the readiness for maneuvers to avoid accident. For we will ponder what to do when vision is blurred or road signs warning of hazard increase in frequency, variety or unfamiliarity. And of course, we can consider the option of walking instead of driving.

A similar pattern of individual behavior for catastrophe avoidance is involved with health maintenance. The notion of preventative medicine, say through smallpox inoculation, can also be analyzed in steps of threat analysis, levels of consciousness to warning signals, risk assessment, evaluation of alternatives and decision, with due regard for ease of implementation of safety measures and confidence in their effectiveness.

Immunization, however, may not be voluntary. As a matter of public health policy it may be required by law. The decision thus involves the threat and response not only of the individual but also of society as a whole. As a result, by 1977 smallpox was declared totally eliminated worldwide; only cases associated with a laboratory accident in England have occurred since. Childhood diseases and poliomyelitis have been largely eradicated. Malaria has been dealt with effectively, and new attacks are being mounted on schistosomyasis. As we examine the full range of hazards to individuals, we uncover a historical evolution of social interventions to reduce risk, some voluntary and some mandated with sanctions if ignored.

Again, consider the automobile analogy in this broader societal setting. With the auto, we recognize the role of driver in deciding how to avoid collisions. But equally important are safety regulations imposed by society. These involve highway design, vehicle design, driver licensing, auto inspection, speed limits and a host of legally imposed traffic constraints. Extending the analogy now to the community level, we think of policy—its implementation and relevant decisions—as the steering apparatus of government, coupled as closely as a car and its driver. In that context, we shall later examine strategies for collective security in the same terms we have just outlined for personal safety of an auto driver. The driver seeks, and uses, all possible information to avoid hazard. What does this say about the seemingly deafness (or blindness) of policy makers to signals about the future?

Social and Technological Risk Abatement

The example of immunization, incidentally, defines a fundamental pattern. In response to threats of a disease vector, two sets of inventions were involved. The first was technical; the second, social. First, of course, was the medical discovery of cause and steps for prevention of smallpox. Then came the introduction of public health measures, including sanctions, as a social technique for enhancing collective security.

These technical–social couplets can be found introduced throughout human history to meet all the classical perils outlined earlier. To tribes depending upon gathering berries or hunting, finding adequate supplies of food was surely uncertain and death from hunger a significant risk. Agriculture met that hazard. Technological inventions of different degrees of sophistication made possible irrigation, plowing, planting and harvesting. But associated with that purely technical response were social inventions having to do with the organization of labor and of urban society. With irrigation, incidentally, came inventions of geometry and surveying, along with social rules dealing with land use and ownership. As surpluses occurred from agriculture it was possible to organize on a larger scale with development of military forces and political government. Similar technical–social couplings link astronomy and religion; arithmetic and taxation; money and trade; new advances in military arms and nation building; ships capable of being steered and exploration; printing and education; the steam engine and industrial management—and economic processes of capitalism.

Over the interval of recorded history, one after another development was motivated and deployed to protect the individual against bodily harm, but also against psychological harm by disenfranchisement of human rights. Cultures and religions brought forth both implicit and explicit rules for living with risk reduction before and after death, and these became formulated in law, at least as far back as Hammurabi, as measures for individual security. The community, however, became the vehicle.

Thus, each purely technical advance brought about a corresponding social innovation. Each social advance superposed a layer of custom or law on predecessors so that the recent burden of new legislation, administrative rules and regulations contributes to the complexity of social behavior at an ever-increasing rate. These formal rules of the game comprise what we may call social management.

As we trace this development, a major point is that collective security was purchased at the cost of individual freedom of choice.

For survival, while preserving basic freedoms, we are confronted with the need for a social management of technology. As we shall see, we have had some close shaves.

Case Studies: Recent Rehearsals and Close Shaves

In linking a new order of social risk with public policy, an operational definition of the latter may be helpful. Amidst an abundance of scholarly interpretations, Dolbeare's[27] terse statement may serve best: "Public policy is what governments do." What, then, has the United States government done in looking ahead to prevent some of the perils listed earlier? What can we learn about policy initiatives that both demonstrate the quality of their performance and reveal something about the health of the policy system itself?

In what follows, we deal with three situations. The first concerns anticipation of and response to credible threats to physical survival. Examples are sketched of the partial nuclear test ban of 1963; of military intelligence on technology related to World War II and to the Cuban missile crisis; and of more recent environmental hazards. The second situation concerns threats to social survival, using as examples the American sagas of threats to freedom involving Joseph McCarthy and Richard Nixon. In the third class of situations, cases are discussed where levels of threat were undiscerned or misunderstood, so that in hindsight we can identify unwanted consequences that could have been mitigated by stronger imagination or systematic study leading to alternative actions. Cases include the U.S. government-subsidized highway network, the American supersonic air transport development which was aborted, and the British–French SST that went ahead.

All represent rehearsals, some with close shaves, in dealing with the threat horizon portrayed earlier.

In the first category, the partial nuclear test ban of 1963 is a dramatic case in point. Threats to human safety emerged by 1950 from continued testing of nuclear weapons in the atmosphere and oceans, and possible ill effects from testing in outer space. Evidence had been mounting that above-ground nuclear explosions were loading the natural environment with radioisotopes whose physiological effects were likely to produce cancer in those directly exposed and perhaps to induce genetic mutations in those unborn. Since long time intervals were required for radioactive poisons to fall out naturally from the atmosphere, repeated testing increased the load and duration of lethal material. As to the marine environment, direct testing in the ocean or its reception of particles from the air could induce dangerous substances in the marine food chain, so that, even with its enormous volume, the sea could no longer provide a limitless receptacle for such lethal garbage. Professionals working in the field were concerned about the growing hazard. So was the public as it became informed and frightened about the uncertainties.

There was also a second issue to be met: the question as to whether unfettered testing promoted continuous development of new weapons, destabilizing the balance of terror, increasing chances of a nuclear exchange, and imposing an exponentially rising economic burden in return for only illusions of security.

The three major powers then possessing nuclear weapons were aware of these hazards. Discussions led to drafting and ratification of a treaty to limit all future tests to underground.(28)

Involved in this act was the collective anticipation of grave consequences, the formulation of preventative courses of action, and the forging of collective agreement that would diminish the peril. What was truly remarkable was the relatively short time interval between perception of danger and a move to safety, and the successful negotiation of agreement between two nations sharply at odds over ideology, but, even more significantly, in a strenuous contest for world power.

This is a dramatic example of successful technology assessment, a label now applied to the concept of anticipatory protective reaction. Nevertheless, that achievement must now be qualified. For one thing, as more nations joined the nuclear club, each felt that it must catch up in technology. Thus France, China and India proceeded with atmospheric testing, refusing to sign the test ban treaty.

This nuclear weapons episode brings to mind the more general example of military preparedness. Here, we discover systematic elements of vigilance, contingency planning for a wide repertoire of surprises from potential enemies, and an investment in military resources to counter such threats. Dexterity in military intelligence is crucial to reduce temptations of potential aggressors as well as to reduce damage from surprise. The cost of weak intelligence and misinterpretation was amply demonstrated in the 1973 Arab–Israeli war.

In World War II, the benefits of strong British intelligence in saving the nation from early defeat by Adolf Hitler have been well documented, especially in meeting the threat of radio guided bombers and later of missiles. Such intelligence also helped the allies to set back the primitive German research on nuclear weapons. Utilization of high altitude aerial photography to detect and permit intervention in the 1962 Russian missile build-up in Cuba is a second striking example of both a close shave and the critical role of military intelligence as anticipatory protective reaction.[29]

War planning goes on continuously. Developing tactics and strategies in advance of conflict, and rehearsals through war games, are both deterrents and techniques to reduce losses. During peace time, armed services have the time, resources and inclination to engage in such exercises at very low additional cost.

Finally, the potential effectiveness of military operations is heavily conditioned by availability of material and human reserves. Once action is begun, it is routine strategy to position such reserves for swift commitment as events unfold. Given the new speed of military action conferred by communication and missile technology, time that was once available to mount a credible response has disappeared.

These three elements of vigilance, contingency planning and maintenance of reserve resources are so widely adopted as a triad of survival mechanisms to meet military threats as to be taken for granted. A challenging enigma for survival is the absence of a corresponding strategy to deal with threats of a nonmilitary character.

All of these cases have common characteristics: anticipatory actions were based on statistically credible and widely appreciated threats.

Until very recently, it is much more difficult to uncover situations where imagination as to credible risks, vigilance, analysis, public perception and political action combined to prevent what might have happened. We have all become aware of the unwitting applications of technology that destroy the natural environment, waste nonrenewable resources, disrupt spontaneous renewal of living resources and introduce toxic substances into the human environment. People now recognize that forests have been denuded and only scantily replanted. Some species of wildlife, such as the carrier pigeon, have been wiped out completely and others, such as dolphins, currently endangered. Fishing stocks have been depleted. Some airsheds have been so loaded with pollutants as to induce serious health hazards. Freshwater supplies were treated as convenient sewers.

These perceptions led to a major shift in social values and to a commitment to reverse these trends. Then came a phalanx of political actions. Corrective and preventative legislation was enacted dealing with water and air quality, and with substances inimical to human health. Massive legislation has been passed in the United States for occupational safety and health. Of special importance is the National Environmental Policy Act of 1969 in which section 102(2)C required preparation of environmental impact statements—assessments of proposed technological initiatives so as to anticipate more explicitly possible adverse consequences. As elaborated later, in 1972 the U.S. Congress established an advisory Office of Technology Assessment for more general early warning.

The nation is adopting a forward look. But, as discussed later, it may not be yet focused on major targets or endowed with sufficient foresight or political energies to meet a new era of global hazards.

To return to a second category of close shaves in qualitatively different situations, we examine threats and policy level response to preservation of freedom. In the early 1950s most observers agree that a marsh gas of suppressed liberties had been released by irresponsible acts of one Senator, Joseph McCarthy, bolstered by a mood of anxiety about the Communist menace and allegations of internal treachery. A sequence of official acts was triggered that, if continued, were sure to erode the ideals and constitutional guarantees to which the United States had been dedicated. While delayed, a healthy reaction to these signals corrected the trend.

Watergate represents another close shave for constitutional government. In a tape recording of September 1972, President Nixon discussed his political enemies. After noting that he had not used the power of the FBI or Justice Department in the first four years to intimidate or punish his political opponents, especially the press, he stated that "things are going to change now." Thus, he apparently planned to operationalize a philosophy that "winning isn't everything; it's the only thing." The strength of the American presidency exacts enormous commitments of personal energy and purpose, but it carries with it seeds of destruction from imperatives of political power. The constitutional checks and balances, embroidered by episodic reforms, tend to protect the democratic nations against this type of threat. But the mechanism is not automatic and will not function without sensitive monitoring of and a continuing commitment by the electorate to high character in public officials.

As enigmas of modern government are examined later in this book, it becomes evident that social and intellectual complexity, confusion and discord may pose a political choice between constitutional liberties and tempting security promised by an authoritarian, charismatic leader even at the cost of repression. Observers such as Brzezinski[(30)] see the majority prepared to surrender freedom in the interest of purposeful leadership. The primary antidote so far has been the high visibility of currents operating in American society, including openness forced on the government and the President. Electronic mass communications dramatize these regularly by exposing discrepancies between political goals and practice. But without public interest in balancing immediate gratification against the longer run, this is a fragile safeguard.

It could be said that concern for freedom is limited to Western democracies. At least in terms of practice, a minority of peoples around the globe enjoy and defend these principles. But one finds from writings of Soviet citizens Sakharov and Solzhenitsyn that the hunger for freedom is strong and enduring even in a nation that has attempted to suppress it for half a century.[(31)]

There is a third class of rehearsals for disaster where hindsight has revealed unexpected and unwanted consequences, largely for want of vision. An example is creation of the American highway system. This network of first class roads now links all the contiguous states and metropolitan areas. They afford safe and rapid transportation for both freight and passengers. Autoists may drive from coast to coast without encountering a traffic signal. Conspicuous as are these benefits, there have been serious costs. First, demographic trends were accelerated; rural populations migrated more readily to metropolitan centers, and as these centers then lost quality, those who could afford to escaped to dormitories in the suburbs. The social as well as economic costs to the cities are incalculable.

A second side effect of the highways, but more subject to causal analysis, has been demise of the railroads. As one indication, ubiquitous passenger service in 1920 was reflected by operation of 20,000 scheduled trains. By 1972 that dropped to roughly 300. In 1978, federally subsidized Amtrak, created to rescue passenger service, announced plans for more cutbacks. In carrying freight, most lines suffer from interstate trucking competition and many continue on the verge of collapse. When the federal highway trust fund was being debated before Congress, witnesses of all persuasions seemed compulsive in support of the tantalizing prospect of the highway network. Nowhere was there evidence of thoughtful, imaginative inquiry as to future consequences. Nor was there even self-serving lobbying by special interests who would manifestly be hurt. Transportation as a multi-modal system was neglected. And little thought was accorded impact of auto traffic streaming into cities as to congestion, parking requirements and effects on urban transport systems of buses and subways. Now, we play catch up at enormous cost, often futile in correcting the errors of the past.

The delight of Robert Moses in extruding ever more concrete ribbons and his popular acclaim epitomize the tragedy of narrow gage, short term vision. This is not to say that no adverse consequences whatever were expected. But the way ahead was treated as "The Future!" rather than "The Future?" Here was the technological imperative, par excellence.[32]

Tunnel vision in technological policy decisions is reflected in two other concrete examples: the American SST (voted *nay*) and the French–British Concorde (voted *aye*). In the first case, the dust has now settled and the battle cries stilled so that post-mortem examination reveals that the right decision was made, even though the opponents did not base their challenge on a foresighted questioning of the effectiveness of the project in meeting current needs. In the case of Concorde, passenger flights became regularly scheduled in 1976, but the balance sheet of economic, environmental and political implications already suggests it may prove to have been a costly blunder.

One conclusion is evident, however, about both situations. The go-ahead and the cut-off were political decisions—not economic, social, technological or environmental.[33] And they signal dramatic potential weaknesses in technological choice that reflect urgent needs to deal with the social decision process.

As to the SST, the seeds of a technical feasibility study were planted early in the Kennedy Administration, and the momentum to proceed through design, construction and test of two prototypes was ratcheted in two succeeding administrations, with presidential blessings. The project was unprecedented in its mix of public and private goals, collaboration and cost sharing. But it was severely strained by the project's magnitude, high risk, technical and market uncertainties.

Proponents argued that speed had historically been the indicator of transportation progress. National prestige, technological superiority and the utilization of a brilliant aerospace capability were at stake. National benefits were expected in balance of payments and in employment.

Opponents of the SST talked of worthier alternatives for national priorities and public investments, of noise and environmental hazards, of effects of large government expenditures on inflation, on whether there was a demonstrated need and whether the project was being propelled by technological determinism, out of social control.

Only later, when in-house studies and outside advice were unwrapped from executive privilege under Congressional pressure and court suits, were some of the facts brought to light. Regarding balance of payments, speed-induced travel of U.S. citizens abroad might counterbalance income from foreign aircraft sales. On economics, military experience suggested production costs up to three times the estimates. As to demand, cost recovery was likely to require a production run of 300 copies, yet the airlines never evinced enthusiasm for the SST aircraft because of difficulty in filling seats and paying for Jumbo jets already ordered. Projections of traffic assumed supersonic jets would replace most slower craft, without review of water versus land routings, suitable airport runways and terminals. The question of excessive takeoff and landing noise was raised but not followed up by needed research and development.

White House studies urging caution were suppressed by President Nixon. Then, as the Congressional debate reached its climax, the President felt obliged to fight hard to meet a public concern over unemployment. His frantic last-minute blitz of lobbying involved his presidential science advisor, pressure on five airlines who had been cool to the project and an instant coalition of business and labor raising $350,000 for full page ads and a campaign of high-pressure tactics. At stake was the President's prestige.

Opponents then mounted a counteroffensive, also not notable for verifiable facts, rushing in unevaluated scientific opinions on cancer hazards from possible disruptions of stratospheric ozone that filtered out harmful ultraviolet radiation from the sun.

In that counter lobbying, a map was circulated in Congress showing that only seven states could benefit from SST construction; 43 would lay out more in taxes than they would receive. More than any other factor, this meat and potatoes argument probably tipped the vote.

With that frenzy, almost completely overlooked was the limited scope of the decision step to fund only two prototype aircraft, not to subsidize a large fleet. But also missed was the fact that fuel requirements of an SST fleet equalled ten percent of the nation's petroleum consumption. And, finally, it was revealed that the state of the art for supersonic passenger flight was so immature that the Boeing Company that won the design competition had to jettison its own concept in favor of the model that lost.

The clumsy, harsh tactics that distinguished the hysterical final days exhausted the contenders, left a bitter taste with all participants, did not enlighten the electorate and shook the political theatre that staged one of the most important public acts of deciding on technology-related policy. Experts, incidentally, joined the fray on both sides, but objectivity was seriously blurred in a confusion of political noise and hot advocacy. Indeed, the public witnessed government as a strong-arm promoter, unable to fulfill the role of trustee of the public interest.

In retrospect, this American decision to cancel seems wise. It was decided, however, not by well-knit judgments based on fact, nor on assessment of risk, uncertainty and costs to those not directly involved. The decision was, and had to be, political. But it was close. It was a lesson in what happens when timing of anticipatory analysis comes too late and too close to the biting of political bullets.

An exposé of the British–French Concorde development reveals a similar pattern of SST advocacy, but in a political environment that suppressed debate.[(34)] Here, the stubborn insistence to proceed entails a subsidy that may prove so expensive as to wipe out anticipated benefits and reveal that the affirmative decision was just plain wrong.

It is against this perspective of rehearsals and close shaves that in the decade of the 1970s an unsettling queue seems uncoiling of unresolved political issues associated with the earlier inventory of global dangers. For six years, SALT talks have teetered with fits and starts, and the number of nuclear powers seems destined to increase. Debates on new weapon research shift from B-1 to neutron shells, but without balanced attention to disarmament. Risks of accident or theft from nuclear power plants are on the rise, with little increase in international safeguards. The population growth has slowed, but risk of famine continues. Arguments stall legislation to begin an inter-nation food reserve. More nations striving for industrialization vie for raw materials and waste continues. The energy dilemma remains, compromised by flaccid measures, with U.S. oil imports continuing to rise. Federally sponsored research on solar energy and on conservation stumbles off the starting block. Only a trickle of surplus wealth in the OPEC world seems destined to help developing nations still reeling from increased pressure on their economy from higher energy costs. And the U.S. balance of payments worsens.

As to toxic substances already in the environment, the head of the Environmental Protection Agency admits that nobody knows which of the 70,000 compounds in commercial use are dangerous. Controversy on DNA research in universities remains obfuscated by local debates on detail rather than attention at a national level to principle, including public policy on DNA research now conducted quietly by industry. The U.N. Law of the Sea Conference abandons the opportunity of a cooperative use of the ocean and application of the concept that its resources are a common heritage of mankind; a salutary rehearsal for a step toward world order was lost. The new American commitment to human rights wobbles from an enfilade of defensive rhetoric, while urban guerrillas continue their "mindless anarchy" with the murder of former Italian Premier Aldo Moro.

Greater material abundance has not purchased durable economic security; we cannot afford more services to match well-intentioned dedication to human welfare. A tragedy of the commons is replayed. Communities lose their identity; the sense of kinship is dissolved. Technology seeks to abolish labor rather than to ennoble it. Even the leisure that we seek is accompanied by more noise, greater traffic jams, overcrowding of recreational parks; precious equanimity and privacy are squeezed out.

These items on the policy agenda have numerous features in common that bear on the theme of this book. Most involve a major technology, the pursuit of which promised clear benefits, but whose insidious side effects entailed adverse consequences. All involve government, and all involve political choice. Despite the widely held dogma that now, as during the industrial revolution, technology is primarily steered by private enterprise, concrete evidence and analysis reveal many different hands are on or wrestling for the tiller, including that of government. To illuminate political features of future choice, it is essential to map all these influences.

CHAPTER 3

New Enigmas

The Emerging Trap of Complexity

Previously, each step of progress toward risk reduction was shown to involve both new techniques and new layers of social machinery. Advances in science and engineering inevitably nurture technical sophistication and complexity. Their applications, mediated by the full range of social machinery, are equally attended by new levels of social complexity. And that social complexity continues to increase, seemingly at an ever faster rate. More and more technical, economic, legal, institutional, political and social processes have been successively adopted and mixed. With divergent social preferences now finding political expression, these interactions have swiftly increased in number, variety and novelty, with associated synergistic interdependence on the one hand and conflict on the other.

Political boundaries no longer constrict social traffic. In economic terms, banking, currency and trade freely cross national frontiers; oil produced in one country is shipped to fifty; aircraft manufactured in one state are assembled with components from twenty. In ecological terms, pollutants injected into ocean and atmosphere drift without respect for political boundaries, and a tanker casualty may involve local environmentalists, state and national regulatory agencies bringing claims against a ship owner of one nationality, a ship captain of a second and the owner of the cargo from a third.

More institutions are involved in stimulation of technology, its regulation and application. Goaded and teased by pulses of technological advance, these institutions are subject to internal shocks of change.[35] More policies are introduced for technological activity and more groups involved in collective choice. Because of needed technological specialization, policies and their implementation are increasingly differentiated. To integrate separate organizations and foster coherence, new communication linkages spring across institutional, functional, national and cultural boundaries. That message traffic involves complex technical as well as administrative data. Then a gap develops between the velocity of change induced by new scientific knowledge and a subconscious natural pace of human activity. While such knowledge grows, ignorance does not diminish; memory and human cognition are outflanked by a torrent of specialized information.

A further example may settle any lingering doubts as to growth in complexity. Development of offshore petroleum reserves may appear to entail only a simple contractual relationship between the U.S. government that acts as steward for common property, outer continental shelf resources and the oil companies that bid for leases to explore and exploit the resource. But now the speed of that development is driven by policies of oil independence for reasons of national security and improved balance of payments. OCS development is then found interlocked with a more comprehensive domestic energy policy, with questions of environmental protection from oil spills and with involvement of coastal states potentially impacted by contiguous offshore activity. In failing to win energy independence over the 1973–8 time span, OCS policy is further tied to questions of foreign policy, of maintaining order in the Middle East with arms sales to Saudi Arabia, Egypt and Israel, and of tactics to block Soviet excursions on the horn of Africa. And these policies are interlaced with economic policies through efforts to strengthen the dollar and to stabilize world oil prices that wipe out economic gains of developing nations, while raising the energy costs of food production and fertilizer. Clearly policies no longer operate in isolation, no matter how narrowly intended may be their goals. We find each technological stage crowded with institutional actors.

Next, the federal government just alluded to is not a monolith. Many agencies are responsible for different technical aspects of OCS development: the Bureau of Land Management and Geological Survey in the Department of Interior, several branches of the National Oceanic and Atmospheric Administration in Commerce, the Environmental Protection Agency, the U.S. Coast Guard in Transportation, the new Department of Energy, the U.S. Army Corps of Engineers, the Treasury Department and Office of Management and Budget; and at a broader scale, the State Department. Similarly in the Congress, some 12 subcommittees have jurisdiction over facets of offshore oil development.

This organizational jigsaw puzzle, incidentally, confirms the observation that issues now seldom correspond to boundaries of a single agency but more and more cross departmental lines. With government less able to cope by simply shoehorning functions into one compartment, integration is required of specialized missions that otherwise fracture and deter social performance of policy. Powerful incentives and coordination mechanics must then be brought into play to orchestrate the bureaucracy and counter sectoral parochialism. Consequently, new networks come into being, thus paradoxically adding still further complexity.

The oil companies themselves involve other networks of bankers; of firms subcontracting geophysical exploration, designing, building and servicing offshore platforms and developing new engineering techniques of oil transportation; of distribution and marketing enterprises, power utilities and commercial customers who use petroleum as chemical feedstock. Because of recent attention to coastal zone management, states are involved with their family of departments concerned separately for environmental protection, economic promotion, regulation of ports, etc. Lastly, the courts have been involved in adjudicating suits brought by public interest organizations.

Overlying that maze of institutional actors are the reams of administrative regulations each agency generates to carry out its individual mission, and which inevitably interact and often conflict with each other.

In raising this issue of complexity, we are obliged to reckon with another major change. Unlike earlier times, when social complexity was the price for reducing risk, the risks may *not* be decreasing. *Indeed, we now engage an intriguing notion that risks may not only be rising at the same time that social complexity is snowballing, but rising because of it*. This enigma is what inspired Vickers' sagacious reference to the trap of complexity, a phrase borrowed to title this section.[36]

As evidence of these contradictions to progress, we engage in strenuous adversarial debate, devise new economic strategies, add more and more rules and regulations to meet multiple objectives, found new institutions interlocked with the old, or just reorganize.

No wonder there is a widespread sense of frustration at the hands of both public and private bureaucracies. Decisions become more occult and seemingly out of reach of the citizen. And institutions of every class intent on mastering these growing constraints on their maneuvering room become imperious, indifferent and uncongenial to individual lifeways.

In recent history, as citizens gained political choice, the economic costs and social constraints to meet collective hazards were considered an acceptable tradeoff of social complexity to reduce risk. Now, as Elliot Richardson pointed out, the problem is not simply one of growing complexity, but of keeping it within bounds of human comprehension.[(37)]

To be sure, complexity is a natural companion of pluralism. However, a saturation point of effectiveness may well be reached where the increase in social complexity intended to reduce uncertainty may be counterproductive. Both fragmentation and its countermeasures add to complexity. Even within government, when 23 agencies deal with ocean affairs, 13 with energy, etc., integration of policies and coordination of programs present a major challenge to public administration. And increased transaction costs for internal coordination and communication may actually be soaking up national economic surpluses.[(38)]

If we accept this as one interpretation of the current malaise, we can understand better why different miracle cures are vigorously merchandised.

Inevitably, the loudest voices advocate reform in government, to overcome crankiness or creakiness in a fragmented, bewildered society. There is a shrill call for renewed economic growth to pay for more, and more expensive, insurance against risk, and to produce and sell more adult toys and artifacts. And there are the softer but familiar voices of reason simply urging more long range planning.

Thoughtful vendors of these panaceas, no matter how varied their arguments, implicitly agree on one principle. In fashioning remedies they all assume a "system" of almost Newtonian mechanical properties regarding cause and effect. That is, each has a mental model of how the system works, such that, like a piano, if you depress a certain black key, a certain note is struck every time. In complex systems, that may not be true. For one thing, in social systems, unlike physical systems, the components do not have fixed properties. How each unit behaves depends somewhat on its relationship to neighbors. Moreover, each component changes with time, partly as a result of the learning process through these interactions. As is currently argued in dialectic psychology, individuals in social situations may be a little different after each encounter, or a sequence. So it may be with social institutions.

Complexity exaggerates the fuzziness of interaction and change so as to obscure cause–effect linkages. The past no longer becomes a sure guide to the future. If expectations are repeatedly frustrated, we lose confidence both in the validity of our judgment and in the processes of structuring reality. In the auto analogy, suppose the front wheel assembly no longer seems predictably connected to the steering wheel. Right turns suddenly have to be executed with a foot on the brake, and left with a hand control to override the automatic choke and prevent the engine from dying. A driver is bound to lose confidence in safely traversing a route suddenly confronted with surprise pot holes. And the trip is not eased by different passengers shouting their own brands of advice to the driver simultaneously. Citizen participation so devoutly sought in a democracy creates its own dilemmas.

With whatever optimism the driver now looks ahead, it will be tempered by the knowledge that his vehicle will not behave as it used to. A society, facing this same type of discontinuity, no longer sees the future as a simple extension of the past. It is ironic indeed that knowledge developed for social progress may actually undermine the system if, by its growth and incomprehensibility, it breeds these debilitating gyrations.

To be sure, with practice and concentration, one might get the hang of it. In such event we can be sure that operations will be far more strenuous and exhausting. Anyone who has piloted a power boat in heavy seas with wind directions contrary to waves and strong currents knows the problem of random coupling.

To summarize, propositions regarding complexity dealt with here are not concerned directly with science and engineering entailed in technical advances themselves. Indeed, any inference that the growth and influence of social complexity is simply a manifestation of the intrinsic technical complexity may be wrong. More to the point, we are concerned with complexity arising from diversity of societal elements interlinked in complicated ways, and from unsystematic and rapid dynamic changes in arrangements of historical institutions and customs. Such mounting complexity of human affairs imposes new demands on all institutions. It is of special interest to examine that added burden on the political system.

The Technological System

Along with the widely held agreement that science and technology profoundly affect the social and physical environment of almost everyone on the planet is recognition that, individually or collectively in discrete organizations, almost everyone on the planet is a participant in technological enterprise. Such involvement is obvious for the industrial manager, assembly line mechanic or scientist and engineer engaged in research and development. Although not always so perceived, policy makers are highly influential actors on the technological stage, in making choices and allocating resources for weapon systems, space exploration and urban mass transit, or setting standards for water quality. Indeed, anonymous individual citizens are also universal clients of technology, whether as consumers of sophisticated products in the marketplace or as voters on a referendum for nuclear power. That attitudes toward technology vary widely is well understood; their basic roots in human psychology that influence the ease of coping in a technological culture are seldom as sharply drawn as Pirsig engagingly portrayed in *Zen and the Art of Motorcycle Maintenance*.[39]

To understand what is going on with such a diverse group of interacting elements, it is advantageous to map the entire enterprise. In the first instance, we consider it to be a collection of different sets of organizations. Each set provides a particular output of goods or services: TV sets, frozen foods, urban transportation, health care or military security. Whatever their output, all sets have common properties that can be defined in an abstraction of a "technological delivery system."[40] This symbolic network, portrayed in Fig. 1, can be understood as a "system", either as a metaphor signifying comprehensiveness or as satisfying rigorous technical formalization. These social systems thus incorporate discrete components, linkages, inputs and outputs. Inputs include specialized knowledge, capital, natural and human resources, and human values. Outputs include the intended goods or services and unintended effects on social and physical environments.

The distinctive organizational participants that play some role in generating or shaping the desired outputs include university research laboratories, private industrial firms, interest groups, governmental agencies and regulatory bodies, legislatures, the courts and the ultimate client of technology—the individual citizen. Even institutions beyond national boundaries are entailed. Separate as they may appear to be, these organizations are highly dependent on each other, and indeed that dependency furnishes a fundamental motivation for collective action to perform the intended function.

These organizations are linked by channels for communication. Information constitutes the vital substance that animates components through market, political, legal and social processes so as to develop a coherent response to output demands, albeit within internal and external constraints on individual and on institutional behavior.

Each specific purpose of consumer amenity thus becomes an organizing principle and source of stimulus around which management acts.

To explain the concept of a technological delivery system further, knowledge producers (on the left edge of Fig. 1) exert a push of discovery, collinear with knowledge consumers (on the right) that exert a pull expressing human needs. The resulting vectors are coupled in a technological enterprise that follows the Galbraith definition of "technostructure."[41] The enterprise is assembled and steered by industrial management to sense the demand; to mobilize research and development as generators of new knowledge, capital, natural resources, fiscal and human resources; to survey the external constraints or impediments to accomplishment; and to innovate, plan and develop market strategies and tactics.

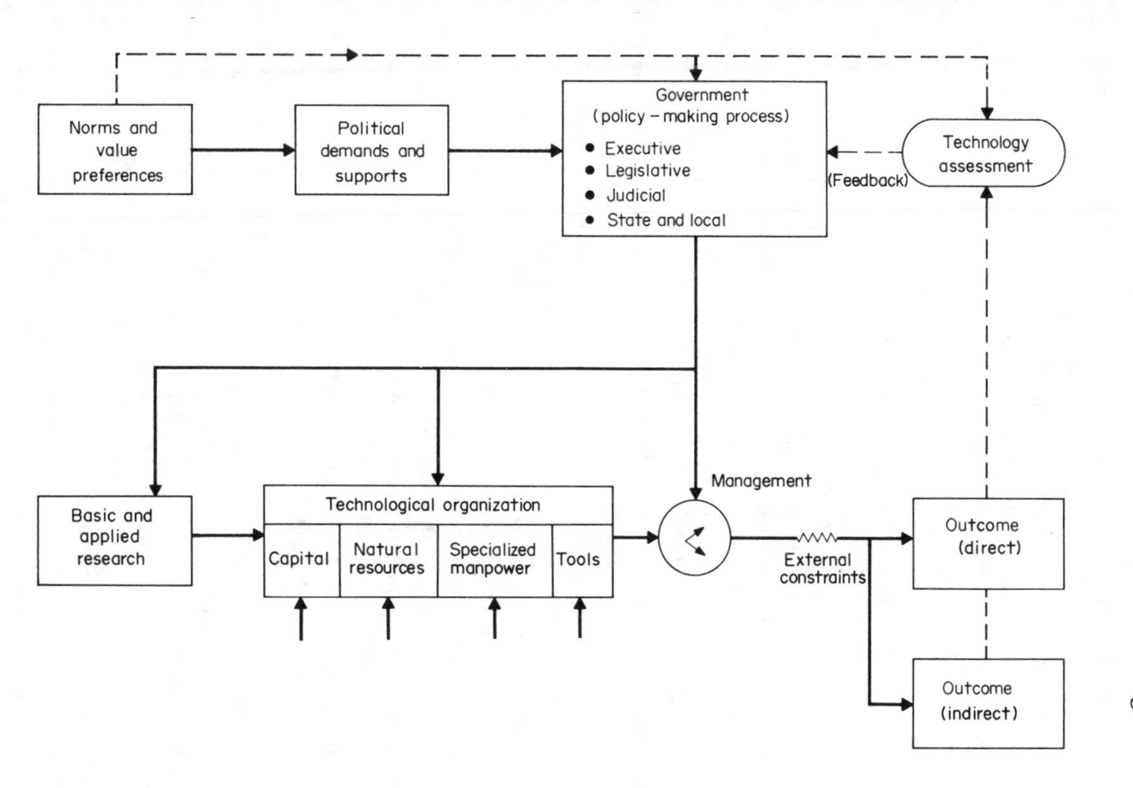

FIG. 1. The technological delivery system.

Overall, each complex, technological delivery system is internally differentiated and hierarchically interrelated by institutions, with separate and possibly conflicting purposes.[42]

Each system is laced by internal communications with widely dispersed points of decision making associated with goal setting, resource allocation, bargaining, conflict resolution and performance analysis.

In this pattern, beginning roughly 150 years ago, technical inventions of coal-fired plants and steam engines were combined with new economic institutions of private capitalism to produce abundant energy, then automobiles and aircraft, modern agriculture and mass-produced consumer goods. In the West, they were and are mainly private.

Gradually, however, government played a role. In the United States, land grants were awarded to the railroads as incentives to accelerate settlement of the wilderness, then its exploitation. Steam boilers were regulated to protect the public against explosions. Then came another mode of regulation to deter economic monopoly which prevented full enjoyment of the fruits of industrial technology. The federal government also created a powerful research capability to enhance agriculture, together with educational aids for the farmer through land grant colleges and extension services.

In general terms, government appears in every technological delivery system, in key roles of authoritatively sensing and ranking value preferences of both special interests and the public, in many countries with a heavy overlay of political ideology. These are then translated into explicit policies and programs. Technostructural behavior is thus strongly influenced through four governmental instrumentalities: incentives to private investment such as tax breaks and subsidies; regulation of safety, environmental quality and business practices; underwriting social overhead in support of scientific research and specialized education; and engagement directly as a technological customer for national security, and now for civil purposes.

Parenthetically, it was the potential of technology as an instrument of foreign policy that tempted the Third Reich to ignite World War II; and the response by the Allies depended on technology rather than on massive armies to contain the aggression. Most government agencies created since World War II have conspicuous technology-related missions: health, energy, transportation, space exploration, environmental and safety management. That scope is being further stretched with rising expectations to prevent or control crime, widen health care, facilitate urban rehabilitation.

Basically influencing the entire set of public and private enterprises, however, are human values. The social scene rings today with shouts of value preferences, put forward by vested interests and by militant citizen groups. The loudest voices are raised on topics of disservice, disenfranchisement, disamenities, and in demands for consumer and environmental protection.[(43)]

Thus we see the metaphoric ship of state as heavily powered by technological engines, governed from within by an administrative guidance system, but requiring public policy as the major mechanism for collective steering.

This concept of social process reveals a crucial imprint of technology in that the character of each technological delivery system in terms of on-going relationships, mutual expectations and roles, is set by the direct outputs to be delivered. Each system depends on a specialized body of knowledge, management as well as scientific.

Some organizational components may be explicitly created for narrow socio-technical functions, but most engage, albeit in diverse ways, in a plurality of delivery systems. But while outcomes define the inherent core of specialized knowledge, these outcomes are critically influenced by the social structure and processes. The settings and cast of characters include institutional figures and their behavior; internal and external constraints of past decisions, commitments, and institutional strengths and weaknesses; and those options under which institutions determine and execute their functions. This is the counterpoint to what is so casually labeled "technological impact."

This cognitive map of technological delivery systems helps to depict the interdependencies now manifest among institutions in a knowledge-based society. It also helps dramatize why it is necessary to examine "the whole thing."

The diagram could be compared to the wiring diagram of a hi-fi set. Music coming through can then be likened to policies. If the sounds are not congenial, we consider whether to change the tape or to modify the sound system. Not so, however, in the public decision process. Policies are generated around narrow goals; and when they wobble, there is usually a rush for new policy rather than to examine the health of the decision process itself.

Interdependencies and Side Effects

As the number and variety of these systems has increased, so has their interconnectedness. And that evolution is manifested in a conspicuous new and subtle phenomenon: technologies exhibit a property of inducing two types of outputs—the direct and the indirect. The latter may be regarded as side effects. To explain, technologies are usually conceived with a narrow and explicit purpose; they are implemented with strategies and tactics directed to these goals with at best a benign neglect of side effects. Yet these instruments do not operate in isolation but generate powerful externalities.

Some of these are unwanted; others may impose inequitable burdens of social or economic costs, or inflame conflict between communities holding different cultural values. Some of these impacts may simply impose nuisances; others may be more virulent and potentially lethal. New highways have spilled traffic into central cities with resulting congestion; people have moved out. Airports near cities for convenience are accompanied by debilitating jet noise; microwave apparatus induces new illnesses; pesticides to enhance food production are found carcinogenic when entering the human environment. The genie of nuclear power poses dilemmas of waste disposal while coal-fired plants load the atmosphere with carbon dioxide, sulphur dioxide and dust. Computers invade privacy. Urban rail lines and sewer systems become dominant spines of land use. Indeed, this list is almost endless.

As one result, benefits of technology seem to be discriminatory, favoring the elitist establishment and leading society to become more economically segregated; alienation rises and confidence in our institutions to control technology diminishes.

Quite apart from the substantive content of these unwanted effects, it is clear that problems arise because many surprise impacts extend beyond the assumed boundaries of the transaction. This is one major effect of the new modes of interaction which clearly imposes a demand for social management at levels transcending these boundaries. So we begin to consider more self-consciously the future and lateral consequences of contemporary action, particularly the element of surprise. The National Environmental Policy Act of 1969 was a harbinger of this way of thinking.

Historically, the marketplace defined both the boundaries of the transaction and the information within. It no longer suffices as a model. Indeed, it is difficult to find any technological delivery system today that is exclusively private or, for that matter, public. Such independence, once treated as imperative as separation of Church and State, is a myth perpetuated by entrepreneurs enjoying images of the rugged individualist past or by bureaucrats nervous about allegations of meddling. In the past decade, court intervention by public-interest stakeholders has sharply modified *laissez-faire*, inducing wild swings in sentiment.

With this increase in number of actors and interconnections, actions, reactions and overreactions, new problems arise in communication and system performance. Signals traveling through the inter-institutional network may anywhere be selected, impounded or distorted, with a high probability of loss in fidelity and increase in transaction costs. It was Aristotle who first sorted out the key ingredients of communication in social process by asking, "Who says what, to whom, with what effect?" Only recently have we asked further, "through what channels?"

Social systems that were once small, orderly and predictable have become very large, incomprehensible and far more demanding of steering skills. Technical aids to internal communication, such as the telephone and Xerox, add information capabilities, but the deluge of talk may only spawn cacophony. Endless scientific specialties, each with its jargon, add to the confusion.

The capability of technological delivery systems to produce socially satisfactory outcomes may now be seriously undermined because nowhere is there an appreciation of the gestalt.

Different elements lose touch with each other as they machine grooves of narrow commitment. Since cause–effect inferences from consistent and clear past associations no longer afford the necessary instruction for steering, the enterprise begins to falter. Indeed, we begin to suspect that the entire network may be displaying a systemic pathology; some observers believe it may already be overconnected.[44]

Ignorance, Blunder, Folly and Mischief

Side effects of technological initiatives have generally not been anticipated. Certainly, they were not injected by surreptitious villainy. In almost every case, damaging impacts are inadvertent and capricious, the consequence of ignorance, blunder, folly or failures in imagination. Ironically, promoters of technological initiatives have not built analysis of external impacts into their management calculus. Indeed, the more advanced and massive a technology, the less the inclination of advocates to consider alternatives and ease adverse effects.

The notion immediately arises, and is treated later in detail, of the need for systematic early warning, to mitigate, moderate, limit or prevent negative consequences, particularly consequences of a scale threatening human survival.

CHAPTER 4

Political Dimensions of Public Policy

Government as a Steering System

Governments have always accorded the highest priority to security and safety, propagandizing citizens to accept the leadership's perception of threat. Enrichment of the quality of life has held second place. In this respect, governments have acted as stewards for collective interests, intervening when stated objectives have exceeded individual or private institutional capabilities. A government functions to rank social priorities, to allocate resources, to organize social, economic and political activity, and to gain harmony among disparate institutional mechanisms which differ in roles, internally derived aspirations and motivations. To do this, governments make three types of decisions: as to the relative responsibilities of public and private sectors, the selection of benefits and beneficiaries, and the recruitment of public resources. Decisions are implemented through political power (baldly stated, through coercion). Coercive style and vigor are set by the political system, which in each culture succeeds or fails depending on public acceptance of authoritarian measures and on the track record of performance.

Explicit governmental decisions are packaged as public policies. These embrace both ends and means—the commitment and direction of social action, the marshaling of human and physical resources and application to specific goals within the constraints of law and custom which society has previously chosen to adopt. Given the fragmented structure of delivery systems, integration is possible only through effective communication of policy.

Thus, information is the essence of political action. Indeed, responses of varied components in a technological delivery system to the same policy signals furnish a diagnostic tool as to how the system works.

By definition, decisions involve a choice of one alternative over another. In almost no case today, however, is this the choice of one goal over another. Indeed, it has proved an exercise in frustration to prepare a master list of collective goals, ranked in order of preference. People simply will not make that kind of absolute tradeoff. They want some of everything, and this problem of "multi-valued" choice imposes perplexing difficulties.[45] The oil development example reveals the superposition of economic policy, foreign policy and national security goals. Because choices can be more easily made on *how* than on *what*, much of what passes for policy deals far more with means than with ends. Whatever the criteria for choice, the selected course of action is ultimately considered superior on the basis of consequences perceived by the decision maker at the moment of truth.

Of course, it is naive to believe that decision makers act only on the basis of some rational comparison of costs and benefits to the public. Elected officials freely and justifiably admit that part of their calculus is the political cost or benefit to them individually, a matter explored at length later. Indeed, the politics of an issue may be more influential than substance.

The multi-valued ingredients of choice mentioned earlier compound the problem. In pursuing several goals simultaneously, we are confronted not only with the possibility of adverse surprise in any one channel of technological activity directed to a narrow goal; there is also the possibility of different surprises in several being encountered concurrently, and some of these may be triggered by impacts across technological boundaries. The very structure of government is thus challenged because of the growing, albeit often obscured, interconnectedness of policies.

Uncertainty about the future is inevitable, both before and after political action. In the face of the unknown, rational decision systems maintain their viability by monitoring any disparity between goals and performance that result from internal malfunction or external forces; they presumably then act on this feedback information to correct the course or momentum of activity. Thus, the essence of steering involves both patrolling earlier policy and generating new policy. Dexterity simultaneously requires an information system that provides a stream of new data to compare with internal memory, and steering mechanics capable of effecting the desired response, in time. This intervention may also entail attempts to influence behavior of other partners in the technological delivery system.

Given the character of this technological age, decision aptitudes are increasingly challenged because the range of alternatives is greater, the consequences of error more lethal, and the underlying scientific facts more difficult to comprehend because of their sophistication and specialized jargon. In addition, the decision maker is confronted by social factors of fluctuating trends, complexity, interdependence, uncertainty, institutional tribalism, heightened pace of change, gaps in communication, and new conflicts arising from aroused citizen awareness. To all these are added his troubles in generating or sustaining consensus, in matching resources with rising aspirations, and in reconciling the uncertain future with the wisdom attained from a more stable past.

These are the *external* sources of difficulty. In addition, there is a second group of potential disabilities *internal* to the decision process. Policy guidance proves unviable if there is inadequate power and stamina for the system to prevail over obstacles, no matter how skillfully detected; or if there is loss in information to steer by; or if information and steering capabilities lose coordination; or if the original objectives are blurred or forgotten. There will also be shortfall in response if the machinery has no capacity to learn, no versatility for rearrangement in coping with completely novel steering challenges, or no resilience to withstand shock.[46]

With the decision system thus so highly stressed and government playing such a crucial role in technological systems, its steering capability warrrants far more detailed elaboration.

In peeling back one more layer of the onion, it is worth recalling that the Greek term for government can be translated as "art of the steersman." That concept, with all of its nuances, has great utility for dealing with the primary question of this inquiry—whether the governmental policy apparatus is deaf to signals about the future.

Decision Intelligence for System Guidance

The analytic approach to decision making would probably be

unfamiliar to most readers. Except in a few highly specialized university courses, making choices is not formally taught. That seems ironic in view of requirements in day-to-day living for an enormous number of decisions, some of critical significance to ways of life and to life itself.

As a result, individual decision skills and confidence come mostly from experiential learning. That is true also for politicians. Nevertheless, formal decision-making techniques are of more than taxonomic interest. To discover common or continuing sources of disability, some form of diagnostic tools must be employed. It is especially important to examine why the decision apparatus fails to evaluate options when vital consequences are at stake, and indeed whether there are fundamental malfunctions beyond command of the decision maker.

The casual reader, incidentally, should feel free to skip the following chapter, although it may be interesting to discover that a knowledge of the decision process is as essential to solving a political puzzle as the comprehension of human physiology is to the exercise of effective health care.

According to students of cybernetics, steering involves three elements of self-determination: decision, implementation and follow-through with feedback or course correction. In government, they operate in a strenuous political climate, according to Karl Deutsch with four channels of information.[47] Intelligence is required first of the outside world—its cultural representation and framework of social needs and wants; second, a map of the system being governed, that is the internal institutional components, their interrelationship and behavioral patterns and resources; third, a memory of past performance in terms of success and failure; and fourth, a view of what lies ahead and of current obstacles to goal achievement. This intelligence quartet explains how technological delivery systems are animated and controlled by information flowing through communication channels. Message content is obviously important, but so is the way information is processed.

The quality of information processing is initially of more concern than quantity. It should be accurate, clear and free from ambiguity, relevant, compact and timely. But communications involve not just what I say; they equally depend on what you hear. Signals thus need to be emitted in the language of the listeners, structured as to focus on their interests and tuned to their mood. Some redundancy is essential to compensate for inadvertent gaps, and qualified in terms that evoke listener confidence in the source. Such communication lacks fidelity if transmissions are distorted or erroneous, delayed, overloaded with detail or lacking structure, cluttered with noise, or irrevelant and unsuited to a client's concerns.

If the preceding classification seems pedantic, imagine the application of these criteria to safe driving, for example, with the importance of road signs graphically warning drivers of slippery streets or of falling rocks.

A second characteristic of policy information is feedback, those signals required by political navigation for maintaining a steady and consistent course toward policy objectives in the face of obstacles. Here, message content must be combined with hearing capabilities of its receptor and with the characteristics of "lead," "lag," and "gain." Lead is a predictive capacity in action. It refers to that interval between present and future during which conditions can most accurately be forecast. It is the key to almost any successful action, as exemplified in duck hunting: the hunter does not aim directly at the bird but at the point where he predicts the duck will be at the moment that the shot arrives.

This question of lead poses a serious challenge to policy. All too often, solutions are directed to a current situation, neglecting change in the social setting that occurs during the long interval of debate, compromise, decision and implementation. Such neglect of change clearly weakens the essence of choice; the future, like the moving duck, must be somehow taken into account.

Lag refers to the listener's response time. As in the transmittal of information, a delay in response will also block the attainment of a goal. Gain refers to the *rate* of response, which can be counterproductive if either too great or too slight. An example of excessive gain is the tendency of novice bikers or auto drivers to overreact when learning to steer, so they zigzag down the street until the art is mastered.

To complete this analysis, we need to recall other traits needed by the driver, whether of a car or a political policy. He must possess memory, in order to synthesize the newly received information with recall of past decisions. In the case of the political steersman, this involves such factors as organization framework and the locale of allies and adversaries. Memory also implies a capability to learn. Finally, in the public arena, the steersman must utilize the abstract resources of political power and political will, and of style in their execution.

Political Power and Political Will

Power, of course, is the ability of the decision maker to influence the behavior of the system, to alter the environment surrounding the decision theatre by inducing components to give in. Will is the desire to exercise that potential in the face of adversity. Power and will are the sources of human energy that make up the currency of politics. Parenthetically, prestige is to power as credit is related to cash. Power is ineffective without will and vice versa. The curious thing about political power, as eagerly as it is sought, is that it can be assessed only post hoc; there is no way to predict its virility with confidence.

Political power intrinsically evokes conflict. The political actor is obliged to consider changes in the external constraints required to achieve a projected goal, the cost in political energy, or the dilution of objectives by compromise, by conflict avoidance or consensus maintenance. In this context, the actor may reveal different levels of power: comfortable in matching the situation; tightly strained by over-commitment; or bankrupt. Of some importance here is recognition by the decision maker that present actions may jeopardize his future ability to steer, especially if his coercive measures are rejected. In that case, leaders are no longer master of their fate, which the pursuit of power promised. These are the risks of action and of inaction. For survival, politicians self-consciously and continuously evaluate future consequences. As we shall see, however, the critical question is how *far* into the future he or she peers, and *which* consequences are taken into account.

To summarize, a policy decision is a composite of political properties of power and character of will, of informational properties of memory, of intake of new information, of feedback and of lead, lag and gain. Finally, the decision process involves a deliberate act of external communication to actuate the system. Given these ingredients of choice, and the necessary activation of any major technological delivery system by governmental decision authority, it is easy to see why the most senior political officer of a nation, in the United States the President, has been termed the systems manager.[48]

While such decisions shape achievement of social and institutional ends and the means of achieving those ends, the decisions themselves also serve indirectly to set standards of expectation with which to compare progress. Thus they influence the long term health of the entire technological system. For this reason it is essential to probe even further into the wiring mechanism of the decision process to deal perceptively with the functioning, and especially the malfunctioning, of the political system.

Miscalculations from Political Process

To understand political choice, Karl Deutsch[49] and a handful of other political scientists have been applying techniques of systems analysis. They treat steps of goal setting; mechanisms of action for goal achievement; a detection system to pinpoint any disparity between goals and performance; and a steering mechanism which through feedback can act on such information so as to assure goal achievement.

Information which we noted earlier that the decision system requires for course correction consists of a data bank or memory of the past, plus a stream of new information that may be generated within the system or may be received from outside the system. These two streams of data must then be channeled to points within the decision system which have responsibility for control.

We next consider whether or not a decision system can meet unexpected threats and survive, that is, whether it incorporates a self-generating capability to tune its performance to changing circumstances. Put another way, can the system accommodate changes in goals, changes in resources and changes in structure of the system components and their interactions? Deutsch contends that health or pathologies of the decision process can be traced to five causes:

(a) The loss in intake, that is, loss in effectiveness of dealing with information.
(b) The loss in steering capacity or coordination.

(c) The loss of memory which includes not only a loss in a faculty to recall information but also for recombining.
(d) The loss of capacity for partial or fundamental rearrangement of internal structure.
(e) The loss of power, that is, the loss of resources and facilities for the system to prevail over obstacles in its environment.

The first mode of failure of intake is represented in those cases where information derived from memory internal to the system dominates the intake of new external data. This hazard increases as institutions age. Since they probably have constructed efficient lines of internal communication that assure effective digestion of such data, they tend to imprison themselves in an invisible rut of their own making.

The second mode of failure concerns degeneration of steering capacity. This process may occur when organizational structure is prized over function, that is, when components are enhanced for their own sake without regard for whether they operate to achieve the purposes for which they were originally created. This is a common quality of institutions that may invest sizeable fractions of their energy for their own survival, rather than for their continued social contributions.

Another loss in steering capacity occurs when the components become so massive as to be unmaneuverable, clumsy or simply unable to change to meet new situations, or where the number of such components increases so as to require a more elaborate communication network to assure that all of the components mesh smoothly toward some common objective.

The third mode of failure involving the loss of memory is the opposite to the first situation mentioned earlier. Here, memory and other information within the system is undervalued and signals from outside are permitted to dominate. Dysfunction then results by excited overreaction. This loss of memory has a counterpart in lack of memory—the situation when new threats arise that have no precedent, or where the social process undergoes changes in state that weaken relevance of past cause-and-effect recollections.

The fourth mode of failure relates to the loss in capacity for either partial inner rearrangement or comprehensive rearrangement to meet changing situations. If a system is heavily committed to one structure or one style, the sheer mechanical inertia entails a resistance to change. In both demands for rearrangement, there is a parallel requirement that some resources within the total system be available to effect inner response. For if all of the resources are fully committed, there is no reserve of energy that could bring about change. In a related situation, the more serious the challenge to successful performance, or the greater the danger, the greater the need may be to commit all resources to meet the threat, leaving virtually none to invest in system evolution.

The last failure of power occurs in situations where limited resources are dissipated. Thus, temporary, short-term gains may be knowingly or inadvertently purchased at the cost of consuming available resources to the point that the system is clearly weakened in its capacity to survive. That hazard is increased as the threshold of resource exhaustion nears, especially if there is a heavy discount on the future.

All of these considerations embody a wide range of possibilities and entail a sensitive balance between extremes. For example, weakness of commitment, or apathy, or withdrawal end in isolation and malfunction, along a different path, but with the same result as excessive commitment to the past. Whenever a decision process deteriorates or weakens because of the informational chaos, it becomes more error-prone. Thus, implementation under these conditions is almost a guarantee of malperformance and disappointment.

Out of this analysis, three notions emerge as prerequisites to survival in the face of ponderous institutions, rapid change, high levels of threat and extreme degrees of uncertainty. These essentials are: operating reserves; time to react; and above all, a base of information for making decisions which effectively anticipate longer range consequences. As we shall see, all three desiderata may be in short supply.

Testing Decisions by Political Results

The only way to judge whether a decision was good or bad is on the basis of results. Making choices for industrial production has the benefit of simple economic measures of profit or loss. Indeed, even public policy aimed at economically defined objectives such as inflation or unemployment is usually judged by quantitative dimensions of performance. We are certainly hung up on the fetish of GNP.

Perhaps at an earlier, simpler time, public policies were sufficiently bounded that quantitative outcomes could be used in a report card. But no longer. For one thing, we have almost universally developed an appetite for social satisfactions that involve many ingredients beyond the economic. Some of these represent fixed values of our culture for thousands of years. Others arise as expectations grow and as new technological opportunities emerge. Shimmering goals seem to move forward as swiftly as achievement. Even a shopping list of goals and credible measures of their attainment may reveal only direct effects in performance while neglecting the indirect or hibernating effects. We could adopt a probabilistic approach. Or perhaps we could take as social indicators a selected grouping of factors which may define the quality of political decisions.

Unfortunately, there are no general principles yet agreed upon in the social sciences for defining social satisfaction or for measuring decision validity. But because some criteria are needed later, three ways are advanced here to perceive what is going on in terms of various consequences, so that we may judge how socially satisfactory they are.

We thus consider the structure of the system, the functional processes within the system and the achievement of certain values individuals want to sustain.[(50)]

The structural view concerns the constant elements of the technological delivery system. These include organizations, major communication linkages, intellectual and natural resources and the existing legal framework of laws and behavior rules. In the aftermath of a decision, structural changes may occur:

—in the continuity of number, size, strength and power of organizational units, and disposition of functional relationships;
—in the availability of human and physical resources;
—in the vitality of the decision authority to cope with future system demands;
—in the relative strength of political will to exercise decision authority;
—in centralized or decentralized location of the decision site in relation to the challenge;

—in the information network as to the disposition of memory, linkages, channel capacity and fidelity of transmission;
—in the lead, lag and gain of feedback;
—in the integration of new laws, rules or doctrine into the existing framework;
—in the access to and influence of citizens and special interests on goal setting and resource allocation;
—in the capacity of the system to absorb the shock of future crisis without damage;
—in the versatility or rigidity of the system for internal rearrangement.

The basic question with regard to these fixed elements is whether they are altered by a new policy in such a way as to change the state of the system in its readiness to function in the future, effectively and predictably.

The second, functional, view of the system dynamics relates to changes in process induced by a new policy in the:

—achievement of specific desired outputs, their distribution, benefits, costs and risks;
—technical and allocative efficiency of that accomplishment, including conservation of resources;
—conservation of social opportunity and choice;
—levels of social conflict and their resolution;
—social coherence of participants within the system, including others than intended clients of output;
—tendencies to alter receptivity to future innovation;
—technique of social accountability;
—ability to look ahead, to generate and to exercise future choices;
—time frame to match perception of threat with alacrity of response.

The third set of criteria concerns factors behind the structure and processes of technological delivery that come very close to value preferences themselves, and how these are affected by policy change:

—distribution of indirect costs, risks and benefits to all affected

parties, including future generations;
—distribution of political–economic power, or its concentration in relation to resource inputs or allocation;
—responsiveness of decision authority to citizen preferences and acceptance of political ideology and style;
—modification of cultural norms and coherence of expectations;
—impacts on human dignity and freedom, and on individual opportunity for self-fulfillment.

These three sets of outcomes are intended to be value-neutral. That is, none can be instantly or universally labeled as good or bad. For one thing, that judgment varies from one situation to another, including trade-offs in these measures. More importantly, the standards for such judgment can vary over a wide range from one value system to another.

The key point here is that technological systems produce complex sets of political outcomes and *not* just the narrow intended consumer goods or services. It is consideration of these consequences that defines "the politics of an issue." At one time or another, every decision maker has consciously or subconsciously employed these criteria in making a choice. What is important here is to uncover which elements are neglected where future consequences are concerned.

These political impact criteria are applied later to evaluate social performance, with special reference to their time horizons. Certain categories such as achievement and distribution of benefits and costs of direct outputs could be and indeed usually are expanded into important subdivisions.

On the other hand, included here are explicit elements of *political* impact that are generally neglected in the usual dragnet of social, economic and environmental impacts associated with technological initiatives.

The notion of explicitly including political impacts, incidentally, can be traced to the Technology Assessment Act of 1972, PL92-484. Section 2(b) states that: "The Congress hereby finds and declares that: . . . to the fullest extent possible, the consequences of technological applications be anticipated, understood, and considered in public policy. . . ." And in Section 2(d) (1), the law states that: "it is necessary for the Congress to—(1) equip itself with new and effective means for securing competent, unbiased information concerning the physical, biological, economic, social, and *political* [italics added] effects of such applications. . . ." The utopian vision of this requirement and probably unrealistic prospects of achievement are emphasized in subsequent arguments that technology-based policy decisions are becoming more political, while ironically, the Office of Technology Assessment, established to carry out impact analysis for the Congress, has circumspectly dodged the sensitive question of political effects in studies it has conducted.

A Political Focus to Survival: A Summary

Stripped to essentials, the arguments so far go like this. Today, everyone on the planet lives in greater jeopardy of servitude or extermination than at any other time in history. More people are simultaneously exposed to common dangers, and a larger number of different perils are occurring in tandem. Most of these hazards evolve from inadvertent effects of technology; not so much from the presence of scientific knowledge and seldom from evil intent, but rather from ignorance, human error and lack of imagination. Because technology is symbiotically and intricately interwoven with human culture, institutions and social processes, effective measures to cope with these predicaments are the responsibility of the salient organizations that synthesize and represent collective social choice—the national governments. Indeed, the major choices involving technology are already made by government as to both ends and means. But in the heat of pressures to deal with day-to-day issues, sight is lost that the first responsibility of government is survival, to be both alive and free.

Survival thus requires heightened attention in the political theatre. Yet, the slow uninterrupted growth of multiple hazards has occurred as if the policy-making apparatus were deaf to warning signals about the future. Criteria employed in decisions largely favor the short term, without sensitive balance with the long. Both information and disposition seem lacking for the examination of two crucial survival questions. In the case of issues already commanding attention, one must ask, "What will happen, if . . .?" In issues and technical frontiers yet to be confronted, the question is, "What may happen, unless . . .?"

As was said before, human evolution has reached such a critical stage that neglect of future consequences could entail a penalty for decision error so economically expensive, so politically strenuous, so environmentally disastrous or so inimical to the human spirit that whatever the immediate cost or inconvenience, certain trade-offs by deferring short term gratification are deemed worthwhile. These problems may be detected as the result of vision, rational analysis or altruism; but experience tells us that political action requires either crisis or pressure. Decision aptitudes and attitudes are both sharply challenged.

What makes the contemporary situation more precarious is understood from a simple mechanical analogy. When a weight is small and moving slowly, its direction or velocity may be altered by smaller guidance impulses than when larger or faster. Today, in the technological delivery system, our institutions have grown more massive and they are confronted with a swifter pace and complexity of technical innovation and greater diversity in social goals than heretofore. Far more attention and energy is thus required to steer effectively, yet requirements for harmonious interaction among institutions drain off a vast share of the surpluses developed by productive technologies.

Some change in steering competence is thus critically required in our political institutions, leaders and processes of choice. Although it would appear simple to identify the key leaders who must deal with such overarching dilemmas and to exhort them to do better, the conditions of decision making in representative governments are such that circumstances may, in effect, be beyond their leaders' control. The "system" is complex and involves many interactions among participants. The demands emanating from the grass roots cultural set are predisposed toward instant gratification that engenders political expediency. Both create a vise of psychological as well as operational constraints on policy leaders in dealing with the future, a form of social paralysis. Hell may indeed be paved with good (short term) intentions.

At social as well as individual levels, a move toward self-preservation must include the reading of warning signs, the judging of risks, and then the action. Social techniques for collective security seem at present to be paralyzed by weak or confused signals, by inadequate vision of the future, by poor analysis, and by indecisiveness. Given the crude diagnostic tools and the purely impressionistic evidence which we have available at this stage of social understanding, it would seem that *technology must depend less on its own virtuosity than on political decisions in producing socially satisfactory outcomes*.

The individual decision maker almost always wants to do the right thing. But most also want to stay in office, to be admired by a constituency or to please the boss. Here are the basic seeds of an internal conflict because these two compelling objectives may not be compatible. Indeed, they may diverge most conspicuously over the time horizon of expected benefits. The challenge to a political actor often reads simply, What have you done for me lately?

The need to exercise trade-offs between pressures of the short run and recognition of perils from neglect of the long generates high levels of stress in the decision process. It may even be perceived as a no-win situation. We know from widespread observations of individual human behavior that under psychological stress, the short run always claims priority. Collectively, stress also rises; we sense a feeling of powerlessness, an abandonment of dreams, and a capitulation to trends, even the most pernicious. Society, too, then opts for the short run. Choices for reasons of expediency become pathological. Indeed, the entire metabolic process in healthy social choice is disabled. Confidence in governance as the art of the steersman is undermined.

We begin to sense that the limits to social harmony in applying technology are political limits. Moreover, stress in the political theatre emerges as the key variable in affecting decision quality. To understand not just the problem but also the cause thus entails the sensitive unraveling of behavior under stress of political institutions and of individual policy makers.

CHAPTER 5

Truth and Consequences in Failing to Look Ahead

Stress in Decision Making

If choosing is this complicated, one should expect to find inconsistent and conflicting, competing and often ad hoc interpretations of the situation; a diversity of unanticipated and seemingly irrational behavior by organizations in response to stimuli from others in the technological delivery system; and a loss in consensus as to effective action, even loss in agreement as to basic facts on which decisions are to be based (as, for example, in dealing with the energy dilemma).[(51)] We do. It is no small wonder that we just muddle through. Scholars such as Lindblom contend that the major pragmatic technique of coping is for organizations to make limited moves in a "strategy of disjointed incrementalism,"[(52)] constantly monitoring and taking stock of the kaleidoscopic environment before taking the next small and presumably surefooted initiative.

If information on key factors is so limited as to blur distinctions of choice, it could seem that, one way or another, it might not even matter. Credibility of political leadership is not long sustained in that atmosphere, however. In fact, politicians go out of their way to rationalize each decision publicly as the *only* way to evade imminent and virulent threats. White House decisions are transmitted to Congress as though there were no alternatives, and if they are admitted at all, these options are seldom laid out with criteria for choice. Whenever they can, political leaders use the media to broadcast their decision machismo and, moreover, to convey the notion that they have kept their cool.

But since the very nature of political action involves conflict, all choices are attended by anxiety. Some apprehension is triggered by a fantasy of adverse consequences of error in relation to the problem being attacked. But some also arise from awareness that the personal reputation and self-esteem of the decision maker are at stake. Clearly, there are incentives to a thorough search for and assessment of options, given the potency of consequences listed earlier.

Psychologists Janis and Mann[53] identify five patterns of decision behavior under such stress:

—uncritical continuity of existing trajectories;
—uncritical flip-flop to completely new directions;
—defensive avoidance or delay of a decision;
—panic and frantic search for more and better options;
—cool and thoughtful scanning of options and confident choice.

The first four modes are pathological; the fifth, while never a guarantee of rightness, is assumed most productive.

To elaborate, uncritical continuity is the classical case of bureaucratic inertia. Complacency, custom, institutional imperatives and perceptions of short-term rewards for protecting past decisions override curiosity, vision and boldness. Such behavior is also characteristic of systems that have exhausted available resources or lack incentives or a capability to enrich their perspective, including failure to seek and learn from past errors. Future risks of change are deemed greater than present penalties of conservatism.

In the second case, with a different emotional setting, emergency warnings are so provocative that almost any motion provides immediate relief. These pressures for impulsive action may arise from sudden menace external to and threatening the entire system, or from internal threats to power and position. The knee-jerk mood induces overreaction to group pressure and expediency.

With neither case does the decision make sense out of the impending dilemma. Anxiety levels are low or not sustained.

When stress rises, as in the third category, there may be a no-win perception of damned if you do and damned if you don't. Wherever feasible, the decision maker tries to shift responsibility to minimize personal risk. In a complex organizational setting such evasions are almost routine because the decision site is masked.

There may also be a disposition to delay in the secret hope that the problem will go away. Procrastination is a widely favored political stratagem because no short-run penalty is involved; only future consequences are ignored. Inaction in the short run is no doubt inevitable, but in the long run it is intolerable.[(54)] Of course, if the situation is deemed hopeless, there may be no will to respond.

In the fourth case, if a timetable of imminent penalty accompanies perception of threat, or if new crises appear, or if resources begin to drain away, a sense of peril mounts. A search for answers becomes hysterical; simple and hastily contrived solutions become especially attractive; prejudices tend to become more blinding.

The roster of federal policy decisions over the last 20 years is replete with examples of all four modes of decision behavior under stress. Repeated extension of the Federal Highway Trust Fund with neglect of urban mass transit and intercity passenger trains falls into the first category. So did uncritical concentration of federal funds on development of nuclear power to the exclusion of other energy sources. The second mode is exemplified by hasty enactment of certain environmental laws, requiring, for example, return of rivers to a zero pollution condition, or the massive, uncritical funding of cancer research. Delays in dealing with energy policy, health care delivery, and world hunger fit the third class of decision paralysis. Overreaction to generate a massive space program in 1958 represents the fourth class.

On the other hand, creation of the Comsat Corporation for commercial communication with space satellite relays is a good example of a reasoned analysis and a cool decision which matched technological opportunity with social needs.

It is of some importance to inquire whether these four tendencies of pathological response to stress combine with and reinforce the systemic weaknesses in the decision process itself as outlined in the previous chapter.

By contrast, the fifth mode of response is certainly appealing. The threat is carefully analyzed. Facts are gathered, structured and interpreted. A repertoire of options is examined and different consequences traced. Resources are assayed, and political will is exerted to make a decision.

What an immaculate model of rationality, devoutly to be sought and administered! Our sense of reality tells us, however, that there are serious, ubiquitous and subtle impediments to that utopian condition. Indeed, commitment to such rationality is an occupational hazard of policy analysts.

Rationality may be defeated by any or all of the shortcomings in the information process outlined earlier. Moreover, there are limits to human cognition and freedom from bias as well as to human imagination in creating images of the future. All kinds of social, economic, political, bureaucratic and legal pressures or constraints may be present, and rewards may be absent for the long, as opposed to the short, run. Third, intellectual and psychic resources to decide may not match the situation, and physical resources to implement a decision may be clearly inadequate to counter threat. Fourth, time may be too short to think and to act.

The Ticking Clock

The ticking clock may lie behind some of the problems in choice. The decision maker, as Veblen has so neatly put it, is subject to a parallelogram of forces whereupon he follows the line of the resultant. He is trapped by a series of permutations enforced by circumstances, external and alien. One of these is the perception that an issue is like a time bomb that must be promptly defused or it will explode. The second problem is the inability of the politician to find enough personal time to study the issue at hand with appropriate care and in a contemplative rather than tactical mode. Both the shortage of time and the abnormal stress imposed by the time bind carry seeds of decision error.

What are the implications?

In Western culture time is readily conceived as a clocking process associated with periods of internally coherent activities that occur in discrete sequence. It is a cruelly irreversible parade of events. In this sense, a decision is not the flash of instantaneous action but simply the culmination of a series of deliberate actions stimulated by perception of a threat, somewhere, a long time before.

As social processes unroll in which the decision and its constituents are imbedded, the chronology of key events may itself reveal interactions and possible cause–effect relationships.

To political actors time is a finite resource, allocated in chunks for varied functions. The policy maker is thus obliged to budget time for each decision, for collection and analysis of data, for generating policy alternatives and their consequences, and for choosing. As we see later, both the compression of time available for rational choice, and the unrelenting pressure of external events, lead swiftly to perceptions that time is perhaps the scarcest of commodities. The resulting stress inevitably warps rationality.

Ironically, the mystique surrounding senior government officials is that these sages go about their business in an aura of unruffled calm. Anyone who believes that simply does not know Washington. The atmosphere usually crackles like a cat's fur in winter.

But there is an even more serious difficulty. With the interconnectedness discussed earlier, politicians detect more situations that affect their power, position and prestige. Then these officials take compulsive initiatives to become involved in every possible activity in which they believe they have a stake; opportunities for intervention arise on short notice and with timetables over which they have no control. To be sure, numerous legislative maneuvers are available to delay or slow action to a more congenial pace or time—filibusters, congressional committee locks, etc. But, by and large, the players dance to tunes played by others.

Finally, none of the political actors can devote full time to matters of choice. Presidents have numerous ceremonial functions; congressmen must meet constituents visiting Washington and help solve problems for those at home. All must offer courtesies to representatives of powerful interest groups, at least to listen. All must meet the press and the public as often as possible to stay in the news. Substantively, the negotiation of solution to conflict takes time. And all politicians are understandably assessing their own power and prestige at every juncture, sometimes in an excruciating quandary as to what constitutes public interest.

Staff members play a crucial role as assistants. To save reading time for their principals they are often called on to abridge the issue papers pouring in. Thereby they become, to some extent, surrogates for the decision makers even in cases where responsibility, much less authority, cannot legally be delegated. The "hot kitchen" immortalized by Harry S Truman typifies the stress situation which is all the more a torment to dedicated lawmakers who genuinely crave to sort out alternatives and to act rationally. Decision behavior under stress is thus a test not only of intelligence and judgment; it is simultaneously a test of stamina and character.

There remains, however, a basic agony of choice. For individuals dealing with micro-decisions, the patterns of paralysis, defensive retreat, aggression, panic or mature engagement of the problem—the five cases previously enumerated—are well known. At the macro-decision level, the same patterns apply. Most policy decisions are close. If they were black and white they probably would have already been made at lower levels. With decision makers on the fence because of obscurity of consequences rather than irresponsibility, small influences can nudge them either way. The last person talking to a congressman before a critical vote has disproportionately greater influence on the decision. Yet as close as a choice may seem at the moment of truth, the difference in consequences years later may be enormous.

The point here is that the contemplation either of uncertain but serious perils, or of long term versus short term trade-offs, adds another weighty burden.

Pathologies of the Short Run

From the beginning, it was understood that tracing consequences of neglecting the future would be difficult. Development thus far only confirms the challenge. Some limits, simplifications and shortcuts are essential, not only to reduce the inquiry to manageable proportions, but also to sort out vital issues and to undertake a sensitivity analysis that would reveal key points of leverage to apply remedies. Rather than examine all conceivable interactions and impose the tiresome burden of footnoted caveats and qualifications, major features are extracted of decision-making behavior associated with sluggish anticipation of longer range perils, or with unwitting neglect of longer range consequences of current decisions.

The reward structure in politics

As a reality judgment rather than bald cynicism, political survival must be assumed a major factor in choice. In the quest for voter esteem, incumbents are bound to consider probabilities in selection both of issues on which to decide and of positions. Shorter term issues are generally more rewarding in affording evidence of success. Other than in campaign rhetoric, political courage or leadership seldom focuses voter attention on a healthy balance with the longer term. This question of political survival has a corollary in survival tactics—a preoccupation with the politics of an issue rather than its substance.

This tendency becomes all the more pernicious as we recall that technologically based policies are increasingly political.

The reward structure in industry

In the private sector the pressures are equally high for immediate performance, although here in economic rather than social terms. Executives are monitored by the quarterly statements of profit and loss, and by indicators of corporate performance on the stock exchange. Within an organization, promotions are based on individual accomplishments subject to evaluation at frequent intervals. As in public life, a seductive premium seems offered in the private sector for the short run. In neither milieu are officials motivated to contemplate the future because they are not in it; any success that accrues too far in the future would likely bring credit only to a successor, and that person may later become a competitor.

Pressures for rapid return on investments

Inflation that pushes up interest rates now makes the cost of borrowing an incentive for choosing investments with a quick return. This tendency is unpredictable, however, and must be qualified by what people guess about future changes in interest rates and their relationship to overall economic climate.

Fretting over uncertainty

A fourth element is endemic frustration because futures are always beset with uncertainty. That way ahead is obscured or ill-defined, first because no one can predict the relentless evolution of social ends or of technically innovative means—much less, of their interactions. Additionally, the degree of threat may not be clear, because signals of danger from political leaders, pundits or experts are often too weak for detection above the noise level, ambiguous, confused or contradictory.

This indeterminacy sows seeds of deep anxiety, but it also begets another pathological attitude that deserves to be considered separately.

Temporal provincialism

Most people live in a village, in functional if not demographic terms. And many of these have no desire to explore the terrain beyond their mental boundary. The counterpart to this mood relates to similar limits in time. People live in the present, and many have a strong resistance to expanding that perspective. As Walter Lippmann stated so poignantly, energies of our society are soaked up in pragmatic acts simply to survive amidst uncertainty. Leadership does not have "the ambition to participate in history and to shape the future. Modern men are predominantly isolationists. They are preoccupied with the more immediate events which may help or hurt them. They are marked by a vast indifference to big issues and in this indifference there is a feeling that they are incompetent to do much about the big issues."[(55)] Sir Geoffrey Vickers interprets this pathological condition as being trapped by a state of mind: the past is no longer a dependable guide to the future, and despite the loss in validity of old assumptions, there is great anxiety and little inclination to extend learning beyond what is widely termed linear thinking.[(56)]

In a way, this loss in confidence is paradoxical, because in a technological society there is a heightened awareness that the natural sciences are built on high expectations of predicting effects from cause. In complex social behavior, this confidence is sharply diminished.

A related paradox arises from this science–technology–society interaction because, while research is self-consciously sponsored to reduce uncertainty in a narrow field, increased knowledge at a large scale has the capacity to multiply options which in turn increases uncertainty.

Frustration with complexity

Complexity of social structure and of processes adds a fifth element to that feeling of helplessness. Complexity, as earlier defined, results from the large number of organizational components in technological delivery systems, their functional and cultural diversity, their hyper-interconnectedness and from changes in all three factors.[(57)] Sensing these complications, individual units quickly recognize that only their short-run behavior is relatively independent of the network in which they are imbedded, compared to interdependence in the longer run. In discussing the "Architecture of Complexity," Simon contends that long run behavior is thus dependent on the behavior of other system properties only in an aggregate way.[(58)] But given the difficulty of mapping the system and of forecasting the maze of constraints imposed by partners and the fact that policies designed and pushed in each narrow sector do not operate in isolation, decisions are shaped accordingly; the longer run ones are simply averted.

Relationships of cause and effect have been undermined by fragmentation and by the novelty, transiency and opacity of new networks. Unexpected repercussions may be triggered in remote districts of the technological delivery system. Not only do simple solutions fail, even formulation of more subtle correctives is inhibited. Complexity can be deciphered only by the human mind—making connections, combinations and associations.[(59)] But in trying to solve these riddles the human intellectual capability finally stumbles over the threshold of exhaustion.[(60)] No wonder there is a yearning for simple, ordered regularity.[(61)] Finally, the very complexity of the organization itself tends to mask individual responsibility, thus negating penalties for having abdicated altogether the role of decision maker.[(62)]

Bliss by selected ignorance

Next, from psychological research, Donald N. Michael contends that threatening prospects of the future will be ignored no matter how serious, if no means for reducing that threat are defined along with the emergency warning.[63]

This condition is made worse by the pace of change, the relentless stream of new problems demanding attention before predecessors were adequately disposed of.

The scarcity of time

There is no scarcity of information. But we may be suffering from excessive quantity and inadequate quality. More to the point is whether there is time to search for interpretations. Telephone and Xerox technologies clog communication channels and distract people from choosing their intellectual priorities to deal with long-term strategies as well as with day-to-day tactics. As the complexity of decisions increases and the margin for error shrinks, one would expect a spirited attempt to invest *more* time in relevant information gathering and analysis. On the contrary, however, the tyranny of more numerous decisions and the hectic pace in most decision theatres whittles down time available to contemplate longer term effects. Finally, there is precious little multidisciplinary integration of factual data with value considerations, and few time-saving interpretations prepared by independent analysts who have no stake in the outcome.

Impediments to multi-valued goal setting

While our society boisterously recites a litany of goals, these objectives refuse to be fitted neatly into a master list to be ticked off one at a time. Not all of them are comparable, and each has its cheering section of single-issue advocates noisily demanding response. The squeaking-wheel syndrome takes over, and in the process those longer range goals which lack energetic supporters are too often pushed aside and forgotten.

Pressures to reduce conflict

Citizen participation in a democracy is essential and devoutly admired. Unfortunately, it can often degenerate into pitched battles between opposing groups, and the decision maker caught in such crossfire may get jittery and seek refuge in premature action on short term issues whose outcome, he hopes, can most quickly reduce the tension. A key role of any politician is to reconcile the varying preferences of his constituents, and the role of compromiser is common enough to have earned from political scientists the label of "partisan mutual adjustment." However, a single-minded strategy of that type short-circuits consideration of overall consequences and ignores warning signs. This is true especially if the opposing parties are themselves arguing only from myopic points of view.

Paradoxically, at other times citizen militancy actually promotes and demands the longer vision. This is the case with the exceptional new breed called social "gadflies," who press unremittingly for consideration of future and possibly adverse impacts. The resulting project delays, tough political bargaining and judicial processes represent a new cost imposed by public participation. Such an increased burden on other institutions in our society that up to now have had no internal disposition to look ahead is forcing a longer range outlook as a defensive measure. But for consideration of the future to be forced only by political conflict may itself be symptomatic of a political failure.

Governments have tried to deal with this problem of conflict by passing more laws. By such rules, all the players could be expected to know and play the same game. But the law codifies already established social behavior, generally lacks potential for and has no function of early warning. By itself, the law may only reduce flexibility to deal with the unknown. The predilection of legislators to earn brownie points on the basis of laws bearing their name as authors may paralyze the system with an overload of constraints and new conflicts.

One final point should be added as to lower level but more diffuse pressures to reduce conflict. In all large institutions, subordinate elements tend to listen for and respond to preferences at the top, and these tend to be crisis oriented. A search for alternatives that incorporate the longer run is often discouraged, suppressed or even punished in the interest of harmony with the management.

Media pressure for the quick fix

Heat on the politicians to discount the future is paradoxically increased by technological aids to public accountability. Television exposure demands postures of decisiveness and confidence, more in relation to the thrust of events than to subtle, long term concepts.

Crises are paraded daily for wide inspection and expectation of simple answers. Whatever predilection the culture has developed for the "quick fix" is further catered to by promises on the short run problems. This atmosphere basically undermines political will to deal with complex, deep-seated issues by appropriately complex and perhaps slow-acting remedies. To do so imposes risks that few deciders seem willing to bear.

Concealment of past error

A long view of the future may also expose the error of decisions previously made for expediency and threaten images of past success. As Michael put it, policy makers are reluctant to admit mistakes, shift gears or stop misguided programs.[(64)] The bureaucracy that continues through shifts in political leadership is especially sensitive to such revelations. No wonder then that political prescriptions tend to be "piecemeal, provisional, parochial, uncoordinated, unsubstantial, and lacking in prophetic moral vision."[(65)]

Bureaucratic resistance to change

Aging bureaucratic institutions are always willing to reinforce that timidity. While all organizations, in and outside of government, are initially created to embody a new idea, such enterprises demonstrate a loss in vitality, a "half-life" as in the decay of radioactive compounds. At some point in time the institutional evolution becomes dependent not on its capacity to sense the pace and significance of change needed in its function or its performance, but rather on the rate at which the organization is willing or able to adapt internally to change. When vested interests have gained dominance over social or intellectual imperatives, the institutions go on the defensive, seeking to retain the loyalty of their adherents and combatting any force inimical to their congealed beliefs.[(66)] They continue to machine the grooves of original mission, no matter how decayed that function. According to Drucker,[(67)] the inability to stop doing anything is the central degenerative disease of government. Given their profound dedication to self-perpetuation and aggrandizement, lack of capacity for self-criticism, and well-engraved habits of thought, the notion of change is always threatening; it is thus resisted. As Allison said, the bureaucracy does best tomorrow what it did yesterday.[68] Curiously enough, the more successful an institution has been in the past, the greater is the self-imposed insulation from new ideas. Policy makers become ambivalent about altering subordinate agencies at the cost of their own political energies.

One must have some sympathy, however, for this bureaucratic dilemma. Sincere attempts have been made at long range planning. In the annual ceremony of budgeting, again the future is heavily discounted. All too often in the budget trimming, proposed new starts are the first elements to be sacrificed. They accumulate in desk drawers for want of resources. Despite the promise of affluence, liquidity of resources to facilitate new starts is nonexistent, and entrenched interests cannot be expected to be charitable to a new boy on the block.

A final point needs mention in regard to continuous evaluative feedback to test validity of past choices and institute course correction, as well as to meet new challenges. Change is implicit in self-evaluation, yet this is upsetting to most members of inherently self-protecting agencies. Of the $26 billion spent annually by the U.S. Government for research and development, less than 0.1 per cent is devoted to post facto analysis of effectiveness of the 99.9 per cent.

Risk avoidance, not crisis avoidance

That politics is widely regarded as the art of the possible reflects the presence of irksome constraints on leadership. Although such leadership is subject to both crisis and pressure, there is a devoutly hoped for bliss of equilibrium. On any level, self-generated change carries the risk of destabilization. Things can get worse as well as better. When the forecasts of external crisis are too ambiguous and uncertain, and when in the midst of social complexity there is doubt about where the throttles and steering controls lie, latent tendencies to avoid risk are conspicuously reinforced. Given intrinsic difficulties of striking political bargains even in static situations, that requirement is even more demanding in the presence of change. The higher the stress on the deciders, the greater can be their yearning for spontaneous correctives and their tendencies to head for safety in the storm cellar.

The failure of long range planning

In addition, confidence in broad scale planning has shrunk, partly because projected trends and events often do not happen. Frequently, long range plans directed to a current crisis neglect changes in the social setting and in options that develop during the long sequence of problem detection, policy planning, debate, compromise, decision and implementation. The notion of lead time appears to be ignored. And the public becomes fed up with crying wolf over propagandized threats such as of communism, and with plans that are shaped around a fictional static, homogeneous society. The public rejects "top down" master-minded planning as autocratic. Finally, remedial measures often prove counterproductive: continuing to add highway lanes simply does not relieve downtown traffic congestion. Not too long ago, planning was a dirty word associated with socialist political philosophy and dictatorial ambitions. A serious conceptual gap still seems interposed between planners and those being planned for.

No liquid resources

The forward look is blocked, also, because resources are scarce. If change is to be considered and implemented, the uncommitted capital must somehow be found—both intellectual and fiscal capital. Despite the multiplier effect of technology, no reserves have been set up anywhere in the system to fund early warning capabilities, and in the hurly burly competition for resources little attention is paid to contingencies. Lacking funds, there is little incentive to conceive possible options which can only become exercises in fantasy.

Barriers in culture

The politicians understand this problem of discounting the future. By and large they want to imbed it in their decision calculus. But they cannot. In view of all the just-cited manifestations of uncertainty, of complexity, of scarcities, of babel and of impotence, it may be expecting too much of political leadership to get out in front of the voters who are themselves buffeted with day-to-day crises, frustrated, demonstrate an appetite for instant gratification and lack awareness of "the situation." The credit card economy so deeply imbedded in the American culture is yet another manifestation of imperatives toward immediate satisfaction.

Thus, we may have to face up to the staggering barrier of public indifference, even hostility, to the long run, stemming from cultural as well as existential attitudes. Citizens' signals as to what they do *not* want are so weak as to be lost in the buzz of action to alleviate today's discomforts. And the policy makers are not listening through other channels. The lack of a common and deep appreciation that the future began today is one more cause of deafness in the policy apparatus to signals about the future.

Clocking and Ranking of Policy Outcomes

In Chapter 4 there was proposed a list of criteria for assessing the social performance of technological policy with regard to three aspects: the structure of the delivery systems; the functioning of the systems; the value preferences of society by which the systems are shaped. Although we touched on social, economic and ecological effects, the emphasis was placed on political and psycho-cultural impacts.

Now, in terms of those same suggested criteria, we may trace the implications of what has just been discussed: namely, the failure of planners to consider the long range consequences of today's technological decisions. The impact factors can be transformed into a list of questions, as in Table 2 which presents a sort of check list for decision makers.

These questions have been put into order according to the swiftness of expected repercussions. Gestation periods of impact may range from weeks to decades. Clearly, the delay in perceiving effects varies from one case to another, so that the rank order is necessarily an abstract average.

These potential impacts are again ranked in Table 3. Here the second and third columns represent the importance the author believes

TABLE 2. *Political impacts posed as questions*

1. How is the decision maker's political stature altered?
2. Will conflicts in goals of different interest groups be polarized or reconciled?
3. Who wins and who loses and how much?
4. Will existing institutional roles and behavior be disrupted?
5. Are new policies consistent with existing policies and laws?
6. Will new programs be implemented at appropriate cost and without waste?
7. Will public confidence be affected in the ability of government to set goals, allocate resources and maintain order?
8. Will determination be altered of top political leadership to exercise legitimate power in face of obstacles?
9. Will the role and influence of government be changed relative to private initiative and the play of the market place?
10. What future effects and cross-impacts in policy are conceivably different from the immediate? Who will be affected and how?
11. Will constitutional guarantees and practices affecting individual liberties be modified?
12. Will maintenance of law, order and safety for citizens, in a sense of community, be altered?
13. Will there be changes in influence by citizens on policies and their generation?
14. What will impacts be on the natural environment and on utilization of nonrenewable resources?
15. Will government be more or less decentralized, with changes in local and state authority?
16. Will equity be changed in opportunity for individual self-expression and "pursuit of happiness"?
17. Will information capabilities be altered with respect to knowledge generation through research, to analysis and to undistorted dissemination?
18. Will capabilities be modified for early warning of peril and for contingency planning?
19. Will government be made more publicly accountable?
20. Will future opportunities or changes in social goals be inadvertently blocked?
21. Will the entire system be better able to cope with surprise in its social resilience and liquidity of resources?
22. What will be the effects on open-mindedness to future change or rate of change?
23. Will there be change in capacity to image the future?
24. What changes may occur in overall cultural patterns?

TABLE 3. *Ranking of political impacts*

	Gestation time of impact	Estimated priorities of policy makers	Estimated priorities of citizens	Priorities of citizens in year 2000 if polled today
Continuity in political power of policy maker	1	1	20	24
Reduction (or increase) in social conflict among interest groups	2	2	6	19
Distribution in direct outcomes of a decision in terms of benefits, risks and costs	3	3	1	20
Continuity of institutional structures, public and private	4	4	13	22
Compatibility with existing laws	5	10	18	23
Economic efficiency (lack of waste) in implementation	6	6	2	13
Continued ability of government to govern	7	7	15	15
Maintenance of political will in leadership	8	5	14	17
Changes in governmental role in relation to private sector	9	9	5	16
Indirect and future benefits, reductions of peril (including war) risk and costs	10	12	12	3
Maintenance of democratic traditions, liberty and social justice	11	8	3	2
Maintenance of social cohesion, order and freedom from violence	12	14	4	7
Access of citizens to political process	13	18	7	10
Protection of environment and conservation of natural resources	14	17	9	8
Trends toward state and local authority	15	11	11	21
Changes in quality of life, opportunity for self-expression, equity	16	19	8	12
Strength of information capabilities, scientific research and monitoring	17	13	17	5
Capacity to appreciate the situation; contingency planning for survival	18	15	19	4
Social accountability and public information on government performance	19	20	10	11
Preservation of future options	20	16	16	6
Capability of entire system to cope with surprise (resilience and liquidity)	21	21	24	9
Attitude (receptivity) to future change	22	23	21	14
Capacity to image the future	23	22	23	1
Fundamental changes in cultural framework	24	24	22	18

is (rather than should be) accorded each element by a hypothetical policy official and hypothetical citizen. In so doing we are not here concerned with the intensity of each impact, just how urgent each impacted party considers it is to investigate. The ranking is thus a technique of identifying what for each party are the "right questions." As part of their cogitation, if a decision maker or impacted party can develop corresponding answers as to what *could* happen, a comparison may then be made with what that person thinks *should* happen. This constitutes a pre-crisis decision assessment.

Some procedural difficulty arises in attempts to order these impacts. Their importance will vary from one decision case to another because the issues are different or because the milieu of the decision is in some transient state of crisis from an adjoining but separate decision. Moreover, there is difficulty in synthesizing diverse views of either policy makers or citizens; the average may not be simply a mid point between extreme positions. But even after admitting these stumbling blocks, a significant contrast is revealed between short term and long term values when comparing the questions that grip the citizen with those that animate the politician.

In the struggle for power, citizens place high importance on their access to and more intimate participation in the decision process. Politicians, on the other hand, are far more concerned with expanding their personal influence and with maintaining convivial relationships with key institutions in our society on whom they depend for implementation of policy. And these organizations display a similar appetite for influence and avoidance of boat rocking. Citizens also may lead their leaders in shifts of social priorities associated with quality of life.

The fourth column is yet another ranking of impacts. The order may be thought of here as set by estimates of consequences that influence the sustained health and survival of democratic society. This is tantamount to estimating the answers which would be given by citizens of, say, the year 2000 if they could be polled today.

A comparison of the four columns shows that neither the policy maker nor the citizen of today expresses much love for the longer term, iffy concerns. No matter how committed we may be to a humanistic image of the world ahead, it would be naive folly to expect a universal trade-off of the present for the always uncertain future.

Nevertheless, given the disparity in priorities accorded future outcomes by the three groups represented in the table, our inquiry must focus on steps to bring the three perceptions into healthier congruence.

One ranking in Table 3, that on "capacity to image the future," particularly the futures we do not want, is so anomalous as to warrant explanation. The importance of this social characteristic has been underscored by C. P. Snow, Kenneth Boulding, Geoffrey Vickers and numerous other social philosophers.[69] Fred Polak puts the case this way: "The image of the future can act not only as a barometer, but as a regulative mechanism which alternatively opens and shuts the dampers on the mighty blast furnace of culture. It not only indicates alternative choices and possibilities, but actively promotes certain choices and in effect puts them to work in determining the future. A close examination of prevailing images, then, puts us in a position to forecast the probable future."[70] The validity of this contention is supported by some historical evidence. At one pole were the Dark Ages, seemingly without images. At the other, as Dostoyevsky has suggested in his *Diary of a Writer*, an ethical image of the future has always preceded the birth of a nation.

The vision and powerful influence of the Declaration of Independence and the United States Constitution are confirmed by their durability and the social and political forces they evoked worldwide. Given the chaotic situation when they were drafted and the conflicts among the drafters in representing agricultural versus commercial interests, elitist versus populist ideology, slave holding versus free subcultures, such a remarkable product could have emerged only from a strong and manifest dedication to commonly held images of the future.[71] Thomas Sine traces these to Thomas More, Francis Bacon and Rousseau.[72]

The absence of images may explain the destruction of Aztec and Inca civilizations at the hands of a small band of well-armed foreigners, the explosion of World War I beyond the scope projected by the Prussian General Staff of a limited war game, and at a different scale, the failure of railroad management in the 1940s to perceive the threat to their viability posed by the new highway legislation.

Imaging the future is suggested here as a major element in a survival kit. People who lived through the depression of the 1930s and World

War II had some such images of disaster. But it is difficult for younger people to anticipate what has never been experienced. Indeed, the counterculture of the 1960s seemed determined to reject all cultural heritages that included some perilous images of the future, and substituted its own ethos on the here and now.

Some readers may ask whether there is a genetic block to imaging the future, given the historically shorter life span of most individuals, and the marginal existence that for eons required concentration on finding food for tomorrow, for bare survival. That tendency to discount the future is manifest universally and may be a form of survival instinct. Obviously it is folly to ignore the dog snapping at your heels while worrying about a car approaching a mile down the road. But staving off an immediate threat does not necessarily preclude taking the longer view, as well.

Imaging the future does not mean prophesy, nor necessarily adoption of a single model. Indeed, that capacity to image may be expressed in the capacity for fantasy, so spontaneously evident in children, perpetuated in myth and folklore, and manifest in creative activity of adults in play and in the arts. Later, the possibility is considered that cultural trends fastening on existential reality, abetted by technological artifacts, may inadvertently suppress or maim these genetically derived tendencies. Indeed, there is a question as to whether the apparently growing trend among affluent couples not to have children may indicate an attitude toward a future which excludes not only themselves, but their progeny.

Needless to say, the ranking by the author is subjective, completely pragmatic, lacking in experimental verification and, in column four, revealing of his own set of values.* Also, it is dangerous to generalize that all decisions follow the patterns just outlined; or to conclude that neglect of the long run for short run considerations is always costly in the long run; or to suggest that all of the performance criteria deserve equal attention. Readers might complete their own check-off list and thus be in a better position to consider later arguments. The exact scoring is not vital to the argument being advanced. The point is, that under the conditions of stress described earlier and the pathologies of

*These rankings were confirmed in two tests, however, one with advanced graduate students and one with citizens of widely disparate age and life experience.

neglecting the future, there seems to be an inverse correlation between the priority accorded these performance criteria by decision makers and the delay time of impact. That is to say, at the moment of choice, consideration would be given first to the questions having immediate consequences listed, with diminished attention, if not complete indifference, to others with deferred and usually less certain consequences.

In the most cynical interpretation of this list, a choice by a president might be made solely on the basis of political expediency when, for example, close to re-election, in trouble with the Congress and the electorate. The bureaucracy and congressional committees are known to push for legislation from ambition to maintain a constituency or to enlarge their influence by committee jurisdiction.

There is another side to expediency that needs mention, however, because the term is now considered pejorative. In a representative democracy, it is fully accepted that a politician will act with self-interest in the sense of seeking to retain his popularity with the electorate. Voters object to indifference to their concerns and preferences, or to arrogant representation. Uncritical responsiveness, however, begs the question of the role of a policy maker as teacher, to move a constituency from a parochial to better informed or broader or longer term judgments.

Today, there is the question of what even constitutes expediency. With sentiments of a constituency increasingly mixed and with a lack of overriding consensus on every key issue, pressures arise from every direction. Each decision is accompanied by complaints of dissenters, often claiming that their representative caved in to other pressures. No matter which way a vote is cast, the principal will appear to step on some group's sensitivities, almost as if the arena were carpeted wall-to-wall with toes.

Under these baffling conditions, wherein lies any safe route to political survival?

To return to the tabulation of impacts, the second half is of concern not only in terms of slow or hibernating influences. These latter criteria simultaneously define both the health and the metabolic balance of the entire enterprise. That is, slower evolving measures of social performance have to do not only with the substance of a decision but also with future viability of the decision apparatus itself, of structures and processes in technological delivery.

Thus, the neglect of the future may not only invalidate a particular decision; it may undermine the future capacity to decide. That is, all classes of decision malfunctions outlined earlier are reinforced and likely to cripple the decision theatre. This is perhaps the most vital conclusion thus far.

Unraveling Kinetics of Political Choice

At the beginning, we summarized alarming trends in the nature of the threat horizon. We should also consider trends in decision practice, as to thoughtful analysis of these omens.

Two contradictory tendencies are evident. In the first instance, the decisions are getting more political, with implicit incentives for disproportionate attention to the short run effects. Simultaneously, there are more and more effective voices in our society calling attention to the consequences of neglecting the future. And in that trend we discover that advocates of changing social values are finding a political voice.

It is thus necessary to examine whether long term awareness is growing as swiftly as threats and inclinations to act for expediency.

In reconnoitering ways and means to improve decision making and to locate targets of intervention, it would be folly to examine only the tip of the iceberg. To be sure, policy is emitted from explicit high level posts. Yet all actors in the technological delivery system share in the decision process, and we need to unravel kinetics of the technological delivery system previously described to see how it works. While some functions are executed by single organizations, most are distributed among several or involve interactions. Thus, separate functional processes that lead up to, trigger or activate each decision event and its antecedents have been identified as aids to diagnosis. These functions are identified in Table 4.

Taking our cues from decision analysis and the political factors in social performance as outlined previously, we have disaggregated these rudimentary functions and then recombined them in a second, social-process model, particularly to investigate policy response to crisis. These are diagrammed in Figs. 2 to 4.

TABLE 4. *Processes involved in public choice*

A. Social preferences
- —Delineation and expression of individual needs and wants.
- —Subsequent clustering of social preferences; generation of conflicts over differing goals and priorities.
- —Refocusing of public demands as bald political pressures.
- —Interaction among client interest groups and delivery system.

B. Psychological–intellectual processes
- —Memory and knowledge generation, storage, retrieval and dissemination.
- —Enrichment of such data by human understanding.
- —Imaging the future.
- —Perception of external threats.
- —Appreciation of how the system works.
- —Learning in problem-solving modes.
- —Influence of nonrational biases.
- —Matching of what we want with what we get: feedback.

C. Analytical processes of policy research
- —Relating cause and effect.
- —Generating policy alternatives.
- —Imaging consequences in the short run and the long run.

D. Decision processes
- —Synthesis of facts and values, impelled by political pressure and external crisis.
- —Functional participation by the bureaucracy.
- —Political will.
- —Influence of stress in decision environment on disposition and competence to look ahead.

E. Action
- —Mobilizing fiscal, human and natural resources for problem-solving.
- —Investing fiscal, human and natural resources in policy implementation.
- —Exercise of political power.
- —Course correction, versatility and openness to change.

F. Time
- —Elapse of time: clocking of threat–response events.
- —Time as a scarce resource.

The static inventory of decision components comes alive by tracing dynamic interactions. These are of two types, the time-dependent, sequential influence of one element on another, and the qualitative transformations induced by one element on another. These interactions are most readily portrayed graphically in what analysts call an interpretive structural model. Differing from but consistent with the earlier map of technological delivery systems, this aid to understanding deals with social decision phenomena rather than organizations.

Such modeling, incidentally, need not be an exercise in theoretical abstraction or a mechanical artifact drained of human reality. Quite the opposite. The construct which follows is simply a graphical representation of the preceding narrative in which each element has an antecedent rationale. The model does not contain, nor can it mint, any new information. Moreover, the structure of the model is far more important than any quantitative data or their manipulation. Its value lies in condensing the perceptual span of a large number of elements and interactions for the purpose of searching for remedies.

Unfortunately, the scholarly literature is not of great assistance here. While many decision models have been constructed, almost all deal with substantive knowledge and micro-actions in the system, not with processes of the system.

As with technological delivery, we attempt to simulate reality. First, we map as inputs cultural norms, social needs and wants, knowledge, human and natural resources. In a steady state operation of the system, social requirements induce conflict because of their diversity. These are sorted out and advocated by special interest groups in their legitimate petitions to decision authority. Some pressure groups may, and often have, campaigned for social changes which did not benefit themselves alone, or even at all. The public interest is considered served by government agencies, operating under law, both to fulfill certain needs directly and to regulate the private sector. Specialized information is continuously ingested, combined with social data, subject to analysis of action alternatives and trade-offs, and disseminated for general comprehension. All of these currents flowing through the system ultimately impinge on the decision authorities, with an associated environment of stress. Stress, it should be recalled, is the one dimension chosen to diagnose health of the system.

Included in this model (Fig. 2) is representation of two antecedent conditions—social and cultural factors that may be considered as biases or preferences, and past administrative decisions that are combined with law and court decisions. These social rules of the game act as constraints.

The component social processes are shown as blocks. They are connected by solid lines with arrows to represent successive influences. These vectors, their position, direction and magnitude, represent

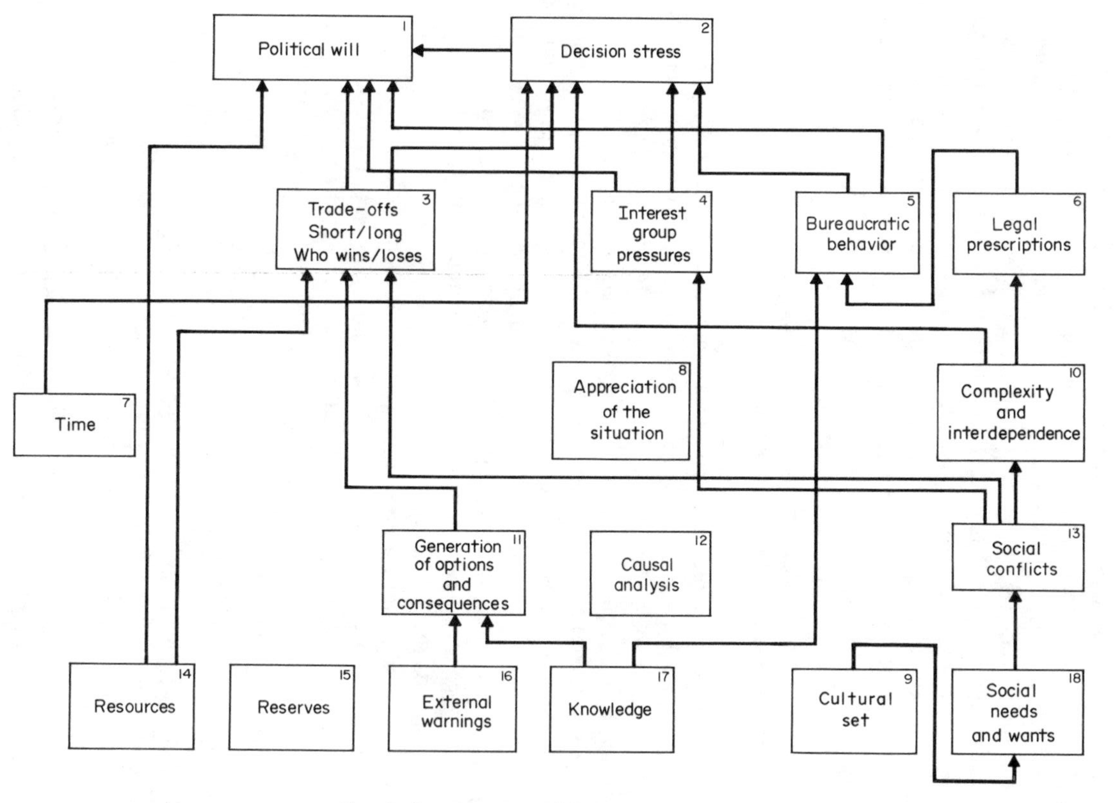

FIG. 2. Steady-state social process.

causality, and thus constitute a primary attempt to decode how the technological delivery system works, day-to-day.

In Fig. 3, lines with superposed dots constitute feedback loops. Feedback may be positive, thus reinforcing or amplifying original signals. Or it may be negative, thus modulating or diminishing the influences at work and potentially maintaining equilibrium. By this feedback phenomenon, the system may be self-excited in continuous oscillation or even instability, wherein small influences are so amplified by positive feedback as to generate an ever-increasing and probably intolerable response through the system.

Such behavior can be examined with the aid of a computer, and experiments to investigate such phenomena constitute a major research field. One objective would be to identify the range of variables which increase or decrease stress, and by how much. While such inquiry is beyond the present scope of this study, the possibility of generating social instability has been asserted by numerous scholars,[(73)] but not yet put to systematic research. One preliminary result of computer-assisted analysis deserves mention. While only 12 feedback linkages were introduced on Fig. 3, their interaction with primary linkages was found to contain 420 loops. If nothing else, this surprising number confirms the complexity of technological processes and the problems suggested in steering.

Students of systems analysis will recognize a major source of difficulty—the question of linearity. By this we mean that the system represented by the model involves variables whose relationship to each other is in constant proportion at all levels. That assumption is almost certainly not correct. Moreover, there may be amorphous delays or leaks in information handling, distortions or impoundments. As was said earlier, the behavior of organizational units varies with the case-specific technology involved, and the proximity to other elements. These departures from linearity for limited actions, however, may not be significant. Precision in social process modeling may come in the future, but at this primitive stage all that can be done is to add caveats.

Two types of pulses may upset equilibrium of the system. One may be a sharp increase in pressure by an interest group. Another may arise externally in the form of a surprise or emergency. In either case, stress will rise as the upper levels of the social apparatus endeavor to

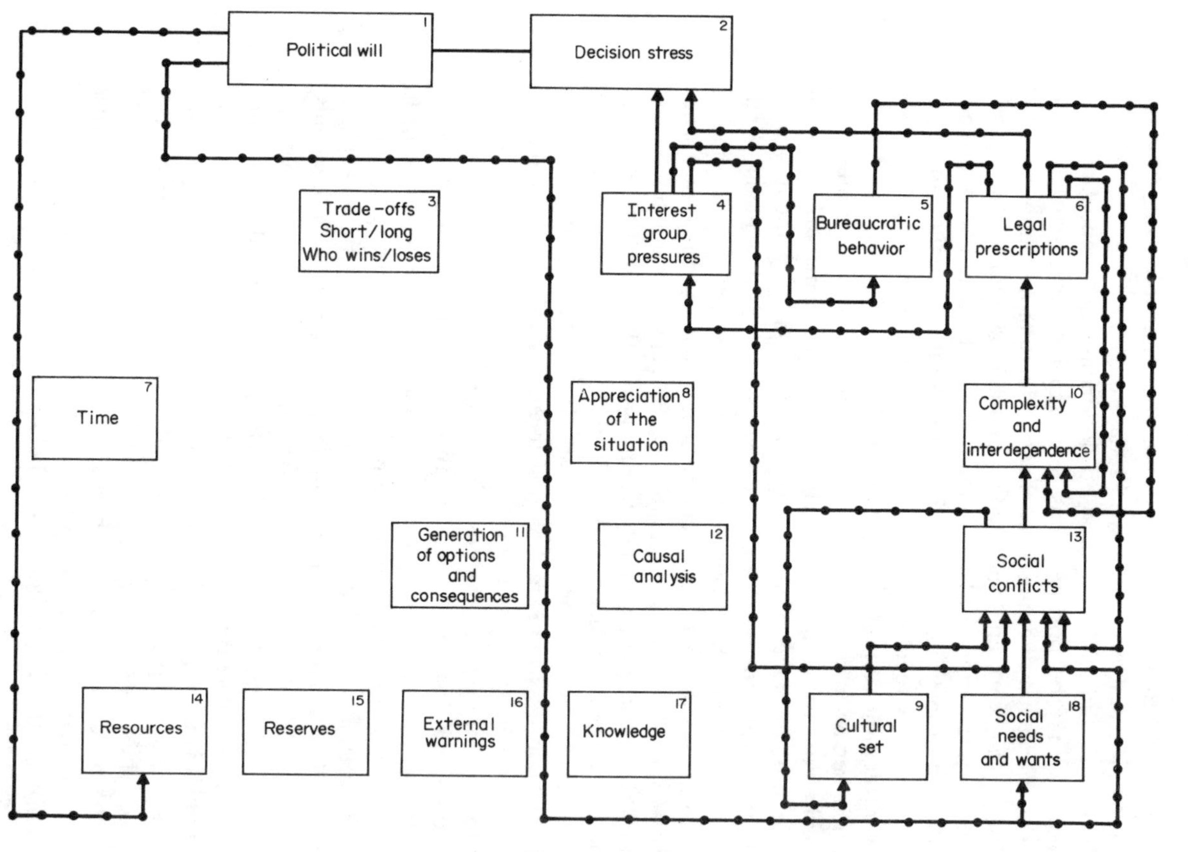

FIG. 3. Some feedback loops.

respond. We are especially interested in analyzing the response in terms of (1) whether the ability to cope with such stress is exceeded and (2) what subtle enzymatic ingredients may be suppressing or amplifying the response. These concerns are particularly relevant in view of our earlier conclusion that the arena for decision is normally charged with such electricity that a further load of anxiety about the future may be unbearable.

As to whether the rising burden on government undermines its effectiveness, two phenomena well known in physical sciences provide analogs for response of systems to loading; both come from the field of structural mechanics.

The first case is the vibratory response of a simple mechanical system under impact. If we load a beam at its center gradually, it will deflect gradually. The amount of displacement will increase proportional to the load; if certain material limits are not exceeded, that response will be linear. Moreover, when the load is removed, the beam will return to its initial, undeformed condition; it will demonstrate resilient, fully elastic behavior. If the same force is applied suddenly and kept constant, however, the beam will deflect suddenly to *twice* the amplitude as under slowly applied load; then it will vibrate. That vibration will slowly decay, depending upon damping in the system, until the final deflection at rest is the same as under the same load, gradually applied. The initial over-shoot to suddenly applied force, however, could produce damage not manifested in gradual loading. The situation is even more potentially damaging if the beam is of brittle material. This analogy suggests something about survival of political systems under shock. Surprise almost always produces overreaction; then backlash and perhaps social hiccups. Under some conditions, permanent damage could occur.

From the same engineering analysis we find that the transient response is reduced with slower application of load. Indeed, this phenomenon presents opportunities to limit damage.

In the second case we consider catastrophic deformation from slowly applied loads. Here, the beam is slightly arched upwards and the ends fixed against sliding. A vertical load is again applied acting downward. As the arch deforms under load, it experiences compressive forces along its length because the ends try to spread apart but are constrained from sliding by the end supports. As before, when the external force on the beam is increased, the downward deflection increases. But with a very slight increment in load, the beam, initially arched upwards, snaps suddenly to a new configuration arched downwards. This catastrophic buckling is characteristic of snapping of an oil can base, where, when the force is released, it unsnaps unharmed. But under some conditions, as in the case of a dent in a ping-pong ball, the deformation is permanent.

These physical models may be instructive in considering whether the political system will deform gradually under load and relax elastically upon its release, or whether it might be damaged under shock or be subject to incipient snap-through under what has recently been termed catastrophe theory.[74]

This vulnerability of technological delivery systems to collapse also has a mechanical counterpart in prevention. In complex engineering systems composed of a large number of interdependent parts, failure in any one could incapacitate the overall system. The antidote to such fragility, discussed later, is a margin of safety sought in engineering design to assure intended performance.

Keeping these failure modes in mind, we now consider a variation in social processes suggested previously by the military analogy. Here, certain elements of the system have been introduced in the decision process for the purpose of improving cope-ability: adding capabilities to detect and signal early warning, to generate causal analysis and options, to make reserve resources more readily available to meet the emergency, and to introduce communication linkages that foster understanding and appreciation of the situation and provide feedback. These new elements and remedial influences are shown in Fig. 4.

The system performance may be considerably altered. The anticipatory early warning and associated appreciation of peril can inject a protective reaction to soften the shock of surprise and reduce overshoot. Understanding can moderate conflict and thus the backlash. And constraints from complexity and interdependence may be relieved. Using the mechanical analogy, the bar fixed at the ends is permitted to slip so that discontinuous, snap-through buckling is less probable.

We find that improved ability to cope has been bought by anticipa-

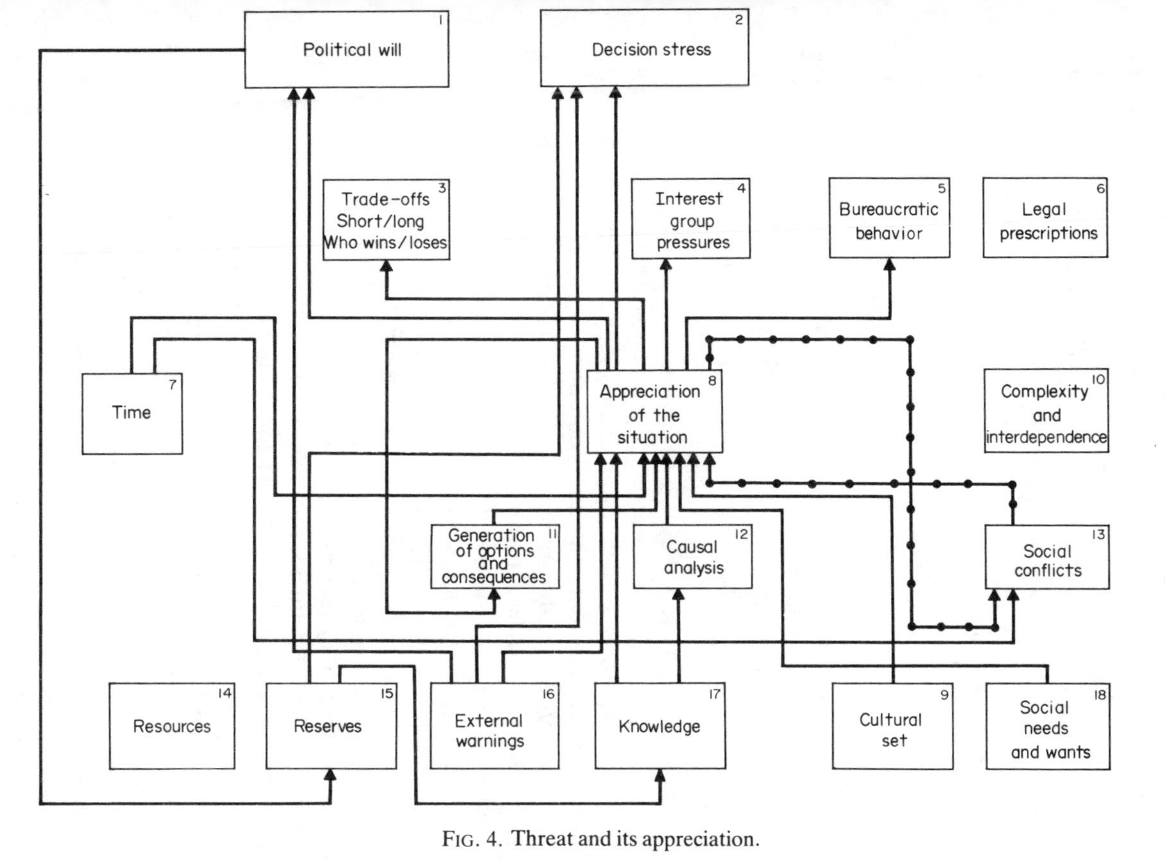

FIG. 4. Threat and its appreciation.

tion and preparation. One salient effect of all these measures has been to reduce stress in the decision theater. While the validity of this notion is not supported by case study or pure theory, it does stand a pragmatic test of common sense. No matter how crude our model may be as a diagnostic tool, a start has to be made. For what we cannot model, in the sense of formalized understanding, we cannot hope to control.

Underlying Causes of Nearsightedness and Tunnel Vision

Using three different sets of diagnostic instruments we have found numerous manifestations of neglect of long range threats. Moreover, the strong preference for short-run results may imperil the health of the decision system to make it more susceptible to all types of incipient failure.

If these pathologies that favor the short run are merely symptoms, their relief may prove superficial. Not that we embark on a quest for a single miracle cure, or attempt to match separate remedies with each separate cause of nearsightedness or tunnel vision. Indeed, we must be prepared to deal with complex problems by complex solutions.

To some, that lack of dramatic effect may prove disappointing. However, we can attempt clarification by summarizing the arguments thus far, this time at higher levels of abstraction.

The theater of the future has often appeared as a special preserve of dreamers, doomsters and science fiction writers.[75] Elise Boulding[76] uses another typology for futurists: technocrats, social evolutionists and revolutionary futurists. Of five components in the latter group, one is entitled "political, nonviolent approaches," implicitly suggesting the general lack of political reality in other genres of futurism. Here, we bite that bullet: we consider the future largely in terms of political decision making about the future.

While the Olympus of policy action attracts universal attention with blame often leveled on incumbent politicians, the theater of concern embraces all of the institutions involved in technological enterprise, and all of the forces targeted on the decision makers that influence choice.

Kenneth Boulding and Harold Lasswell have broken significant ground here with a proposition that we stand precariously in the midst of great transition where construction of a livable and enduring society will require commitment of human energy and enlightenment exceeding that of precursors.[77] They outline, politically, what we must do:

—understand predictive behavior of policy makers and key institutions;
—forecast what is foreseeable with care and elegance;
—imagine what might be in terms of plausible alternatives;
—determine strategic availability of more desirable outcomes.

Whatever the temptation to unfurl banners of a selective Utopia and develop the foreseeable, plausible and desirable, we limit this treatise to a less ambitious but perhaps operationally more critical task of dealing with the future in terms of what we do *not* want. Such boundaries of scholarship, however, do not limit the epistemological arena. The capacity to imagine perils is very much a part of the total appetite of a society for the future, a property C. P. Snow asserts in saying that "all healthy societies are ready to sacrifice the existential moment for their children's future and for children after these."[78]

That frame of mind can be revealed in every aspect of a culture from literature, art, poetry, music, science and philosophy to architecture, consumer goods and entertainment. The stance of policy makers is inevitably shaped by that social environment, and vice versa. Harmony between citizens and policy makers does not automatically mean progress.

With technology imprinting all aspects of our society, and with the winds of conflict blowing more strongly, we underscore the phenomenon that technological decision making is becoming more political. What we mean is this. In institutional terms, technology has tended to concentrate power, wealth and benefit. In uncritical exploitation of natural resources, technology has triggered an unexpected era of scarcity and widened diversity of the human condition. The question of who wins and who loses becomes more strenuous. Because the selection of ends and means is a matter of political choice, because publicly funded projects have become larger in scale with economically more at stake, and because government regulation limits freedom of private enterprise, the social management of technology is inevitably more political. The congressional decision to abandon development of SST is a classical example.

Many factors bolster that tendency. Technology generates more options, as with water, coal, gas, nuclear, wind, solar and geothermal sources as energy alternatives. Quantitatively more choices thus have to be made, so that attention becomes more frequently riveted on the decision event. Government tends to play a greater role in all four modes discussed before: in stimulation, regulation, using technology directly and investing in social overhead. So in most cases, choice is not left to the decentralized, invisible hand of the marketplace; rather, social decisions are driven by circumstances, abetted by television, to high visibility and pinpointed political locale. A racheting then occurs in public expectations of crisis abatement, amplified by cultural trends in abdication of individual responsibility to government. Pressures for satisfying short term expediency grow more strenuous, and, as we saw, pathological.

We repeat, decisions on technology-intensive public policy are growing more political in the sense that whatever the technical, economic, social or legal implications, more decisions are explicitly boosted to the highest level of policy authority.

In growing more political, these decisions are becoming more shortsighted. Notwithstanding the pejorative inference of "political" decisions, there is not a pragmatic, much less a theoretical, basis for this situation by itself to enhance risk. Political decisions are certainly not, *per se*, bad decisions. For reasons previously advanced, they are not necessarily less rational. There are two major questions, however. First, whether concentration on the short run is at the expense of the longer run in terms of adverse consequences. And, secondly, does this growing burden on political apparatus depreciate quality of decisions in general?

There is a growing view that the factors of complexity, interdependence, political stress and atmosphere of conflict may render the system completely ungovernable. That judgment is advanced by Miles in classical terms of public administration.[79] To the author, however, the critical test is whether government is able to fulfill its most salient responsibility by acting as public agent for collective security.

To put this point of view even more starkly, there is an obvious trend in capitalist democracies as well as socialist states to provide for "welfare." In catering to popular demand, the quantity and visibility of these services is second only to military security in importance. In the United States, federal funds in this category now exceed military expenditures.

An alternative view of governmental roles would be to consider collective security against large scale risks, not individual welfare, as the necessary if not sufficient condition of governmental responsibility. This stance speaks to a reversal in public attitudes of "letting the government do it" as far as reduction in individual risk is concerned, and increased appreciation of and demand for governmental intervention in the broader and more lethal threats.

Common sense dictates that no political system can withstand increasing demands indefinitely, although we treat the American system as though it were infinitely resilient and affluent. Earlier cases alert us to consider whether continued ability to make tough decisions, in time, is vulnerable to instability or suddenness of demand, or all the other diseases of stress catalogued earlier.

Information is the primary commodity of political choice. If resilience of the system is exhausted, early warning signals could well be masked by noise. The learning curve of agility to meet novel situations will lag pulses of crisis and pressure. The increasingly stressful role of policy authorities to harmonize relationships among institutional participants and ease conflict could cancel out the primary role to deal with the threats themselves.

When the stabilizing function of government is lost, the system becomes more sensitive to even minor shocks. The sensation, as Vickers has described it, is of a novice ice skater, obliged to devote full energies and attention simply to remaining upright, unable to muster the balance and self-confidence to engage in creative activity of figure skating or racing.[80] As with human beings, defects in hearing apparatus can cause debilitating instability, a form of institutional vertigo.

We now attempt to unmask the underlying sources of deafness in the policy apparatus to signals about the future. We have isolated malfunctions in the decision tree that induce too much stress or too little stress for balanced, healthy consideration of the future, and for maintenance of metabolic balance in the decision system itself. Basically, however, we are led back to the policy level decision makers, the institutions in our society and the individual citizen.

What is required of all is a change in behavior. In our system of minimum coercion, this translates into rewards and penalties for self-imposed change.

Many observers of social behavior contend that individuals change far more readily than do organizations.

Institutional viscosity in government and academia, church and industry has always been prevalent, may even be getting more pronounced. To be sure, there is a positive side to that inertia in that institutions play a role in pattern maintenance, so that mutual roles and expectations of participants are sufficiently predictable to preserve coherence. By another name this is bald conservatism. Marris has pointed out that conservatism is an impulse to defend the predictability of life, "as necessary for survival as adaptability."[(81)]

Assessing vulnerability to the unknown, however, may not be approached in traditional conservative–liberal terms. Indeed, today these labels are misleading. Nevertheless, if certain of our social functions have a tendency to be conservative and others versatile and innovative, mismatches and inconsistencies can arise and disable the decision process. For all the processes to be conservative or all to be innovative would be equally certain to foster debilitating extremes of stagnation or chaos. Perhaps, then, an optimum level of tension between these contrasting currents is essential—to afford internal coherence, vigilance as to threat and alacrity in generating appropriate and timely response.

In what follows, we assume, rather than confront, this ubiquitous property of institutional behavior with modest expectations as to its reform.

Ultimately what is at stake is changing the behavior of decision makers. The problem is not that they will not change; they are in a procedural trap such that they cannot. Given the high priority politicians must place on maintaining their position, power and prestige, and given political energies generally targeted at the shorter run, we cannot expect a change in representative government unless *people* change.

The root cause of the dilemma and its remedies lie in the entire cultural setting.

CHAPTER 6

Coping with Future Threats

An Anthology of Prescriptions

In considering the question "What should we do?" it is enlightening to review what distinguished analysts and critics of the human condition have had to say about new remedial pathways to the future. Michael Marien[82] has catalogued close to 1000 major contributions to the literature, drawing on disciplinary classifications of anthropology, business administration, economics, history, international relations, life sciences, philosophy, political science, psychology, sociology and urban studies. He also examines contributions from cross-disciplinary areas of policy sciences, future studies, general systems theory, and nonacademic political tracts and polemics. Marien, however, omits such substantial literature dealing with technology-related policy as that originating with the U.S. Congress and world political leaders. President Kennedy's inaugural address is an evocative and influential example. So are proposals for full employment by Senator Hubert Humphrey.

From his bibliography, Marien highlights some 75 books and articles of such great merit as to constitute an ecumenical curriculum. Most lay out prescriptions, fitted under such headings as:

—Improving the technological, affluent, service society.

—Preserving ecological balance.

—World order.

—Decentralization of power and authority.

—Social reform to meet human needs.

—Government reform.

—Economic reform.
—Redistribution of wealth and power.
—Freedom from governmental coercion.
—Spatial alternatives.
—Spiritual, cultural and religious directions.

Marien has also taken on the exceptional, bold and invaluable task of annotating virtually all of the entries.

These visions and associated road maps of paradise or of unrelenting doom are intriguing. While considered by some a pedantic form of science fiction (or, more accurately perhaps, of political science fiction), this collection nevertheless abstracts existing efforts to image the future as a psychological–spiritual–cerebral exercise that can be the critical foundation for a hold on life. By and large, they are in a humanist tradition, focusing on the meaning of life and its nurture, and on the individual as the dominant unit of society. Also they reflect the recently accelerating concern with the inner, spiritual state and with the almost universal hunger for fulfillment in a vacuum produced by the erosion of commitment to organized religions, the blurring of moral values, the benign neglect of creative unselfish love and on the satisfactions of altruism. They further emphasize the preoccupation with goods and meaningless, external sensory experience, accompanied by a suspicion of the established order, feelings of futility, impotence, loss in purpose and substitution of passion for reason as a guide to action.

Marien does not find all equally convincing. Indeed, many are characterized as cosmic, escapist, afflicted by neglect of facts, evading questions of political reality, lacking in comparisons with other published materials or uncritical in methodological arguments backed by an idiot computer.

A wide range of institutional prescriptions and functional reforms has also been catalogued, that deal with some of the issues raised in this book. While far from comprehensive, the following list generated largely from his bibliography should pinpoint some of the concerns and, in a few cases, provide a foundation for our subsequent arguments. Each label is largely self-explanatory.

Selected Proposals for Institutional and Functional Reform*

New federal agencies or functions

—National Planning Board (Stuart Chase) 1932
—National Planning Board for Domestic Affairs (Stuart Chase) 1960
—State of the Union Messages Looking Five Years Ahead (Michael D. Reagan) 1963
—New Planning Bodies throughout Government (Triple Revolution) 1964
—National Conversion Commission (Richard J. Barnet) 1969
—Joint Congressional Committee on the Future (Michael Harrington) 1968
—Report on the Future by the President (Michael Harrington) 1968
—Community Planning (Stewart Udall) 1968
—National Services Administration (Melville J. Ulmer) 1969
—National Incomes Board (Melville J. Ulmer) 1969
—Council of Social Advisors (Walter Mondale) 1969
—Council of Technological Advisors (Edward Wenk, Jr.) 1970
—National Conservation Bill of Rights (Richard A. Falk) 1971
—Council of National Development Advisors (Patrick E. Haggerty) 1973
—Planning Branch of Government (Dennis C. Pirages and Paul R. Ehrlich) 1974
—Administrative Courts (Frederick M. Stern) 1975
—Presidential Powers Impact Statement (Joseph Califano) 1975
—Office of National Economic Planning (Initiative Committee for National Economic Planning) 1975

International bodies

—World Brain (Alex Carrell) 1935
—World Planning (Richard Gardner) 1966
—Prometheus Project of Global Choice (Gerald Feinberg) 1969
—Transnational Information Agencies (Lynton K. Caldwell) 1972
—Global Planning (Donella H. Meadows *et al.*) 1972

*Extracted largely from *Societal Directions and Alternatives* by Michael Marien (Ref. 1).

—Bill of Rights for the Planet (Peter Albertson and Margery Barnett) 1972
—Global Communication System (Lester R. Brown) 1972
—International Ocean Assessment and Coordination Agency (Edward Wenk, Jr.) 1972
—Global Authority on Resource Conservation (Ralph E. Lapp) 1973
—Global Guidance Systems (Ervin Laszlo) 1974
—Regional Planning (M. Mesarovic and E. Pestel) 1974
—New World Organization (Richard A. Falk) 1975
—World Security System (Rajni Kothari) 1975
—World Technology Board (Richard A. Falk) 1975
—Bill of Rights for Future Generations (Jacques-Yves Cousteau) 1976

Future planning or assessment functions

—Anticipating Technological Consequences (Zbigniew Brzezinski) 1967
—Science Court (Arthur Kantrowitz) 1967
—Technology Assessment Board (Emilio Q. Daddario) 1967
—Technological Evaluation (Stuart Chase) 1968
—A Fourth Branch of Government (Edward Wenk, Jr.) 1970
—Church for Avant Garde Planning (André Bieler) 1970
—Technological Ombudsman (Alvin Toffler) 1970
—Watchdog Groups (David F. Linowes) 1973
—Learning Society (Victor Ferkiss) 1974
—Planning Networks (Willis W. Harman) 1974
—A Fourth Branch of Government (Stephen H. Schneider) 1976
—Institute for Congress (Alton Frye) 1976

Scanning this necessarily incomplete list reveals that many scholars and observers of the social scene were busy in the sandbox, designing for the future. On the other hand, there is a conspicuous vacuum. Few deal with the political nature of human society or the political life of institutions created to meet material and social goals. And as Marien contended, these prescriptions were usually found advocated without convincing rationales, lacking in realism and without operational elaboration on how to get there from here.

Needless to say, the shaky foundations to these nostrums are a caution to all players in this futures game.

Refocusing the Inquiry

This author is no more willing than his predecessors simply to wring his hands in anguish. So apart from diagnosis, prescriptions with respect to collective security will be offered, albeit with trepidation.

Before launching into this investigation of the intricate web of policy planning, we first advanced the proposition that the decision-making body-politic has seemed to be strangely deaf to signals about the future. As we have subsequently applied several different tools of analysis, under differing approaches, this congenital hearing disability has seemed to be confirmed.

The metaphorical deafness was found to have numerous possible causes:

—Listening may be deficient because all auditors, from citizens to policy makers, are not prepared or motivated to appreciate what is heard; the culturally set reward system does not favor long run considerations, or foster investment of resources for anticipatory or corrective action.

—Hearing may be systematically impaired because signals about the future may be too weak or ambiguous. There may be inadequate early warning and in political terms there may be no effective or responsible constituency for the future.

—The noise level of other signals may be so high as to mask those of transcendent but uncertain perils, partly because of political pressures to deal with immediate crises or with inevitable risks to individuals rather than to collective security.

—Communication linkages may be weak, nonexistent or overloaded.

—Participants may speak different languages so that the injection of more technical facts does not necessarily contribute to political enlightenment. The difference in frames of reference of scientist and politician is revealed in the old allegory when the two are equally baffled. One asks, What did they mean? The other, Why did they say it?[83]

As we dig for remedies in relation to the role of stress in the decision theater, two strategies are immediately evident. One concerns reducing source of stress; the second concerns increasing tolerance for stress. Since better preparatory information and enhanced opportunity for action can positively influence both strategies, we begin a search for correctives accordingly.

As far as the decision maker is concerned, attention-getting signals are emitted from two sources, simplistically labeled as pressure and crisis. One set flows from the electorate at the base of the decision tree, from interest groups and from the bureaucracy. The other set originates in whatever independent, early-warning, intelligence capability the decision maker has at his command to perceive external threats. As far as the long run is concerned, both appear weak.

Most of the actors in the technology delivery system have deep institutional predilections to favor the short run, and have few incentives for vigilance of longer term threats that frequently spill over beyond the boundaries of the organization's role or mission and resources at its command.

There are some key exceptions. In the tradition of Ralph Nader, public interest groups such as New Directions, the Union of Concerned Scientists, and Common Cause have taken aggressive and politically activist stands on issues broader in impact and extending to the future so as to transcend the direct stake in the outcome which they hold as organizations or their members hold as individuals. Political parties in some Western democracies have performed similarly. While limited by their resources, these groups acting through legitimate political process have had a distinct influence in mobilizing public opinion and action to capture policy level attention. The range of issues being spotlighted is increasing. So is the technical competence of these organizations. Still, there is a very limited national capability for early warning, for analysis of alternative courses of action and for protective reaction.

Federal policy makers have been aware of these major gaps. So in 1972 the Congress established a new Office of Technology Assessment with that intent. Its poor performance and its prospects are discussed later. In 1976 the President and Congress signed legislation creating a somewhat parallel Office of Science and Technology Policy to serve the White House.[84] By virtue of the election then imminent, its activation in August 1976 was largely symbolic, so that the ignition switch was thrown only in March 1977 by incoming President Carter. By fall 1978, OSTP was also not conspicuously fulfilling its technology assessment function, an issue to be discussed further because of its relevance to the thesis of this book.

Apart from the lack of effective early warning systems, the political decision apparatus suffers from its own habits.

In a political manifestation of Parkinson's law, legislatures, for example, prefer to tackle means rather than ends, monkey with details rather than fundamentals, dilute their influence by undisciplined attack on all manifest issues without priority sorting. And they are likely to overvalue the shorter run. "The route of the school bus and the price of beef we deliberate with ponderous care and hedge about with restrictions. The survival of the world we suspend from a thread."[85] So we are confronted with questions of behavior modification of decision makers.[86]

Accordingly one must consider how to make power responsible, accessible and accountable:

—to meet the needs and desires of individuals for survival, security and self-fulfillment, enhance their appreciation of "the situation," and facilitate citizen participation in making policy, especially in their role of constituents advocating more attention to the long run;
—to meet the need for vigilance to perceive threat and for capabilities to generate policy alternatives that transcend present patterns of thought;
—to sponsor new, problem-oriented, technical research bearing on survival;
—to provide for contingency resources;
—to create necessary communication linkages among these components for diffusion of knowledge and common understanding.

Finally, the pacing element of time must be examined—the implications of mismatch between rapid pulses of technical innovation and lags in institutional responses.

As all of these implications are explored, we inevitably trip over scarcities, but scarcities that have received sparse attention in the literature—*the scarcity of liquid resources to address the future, the scarcity of activists who want to, and the scarcity of time for them to think and to act because Time as a resource cannot be stockpiled.*

This inquiry on how to steer technology to produce socially satisfactory outcomes initially focused on the political mechanics of government as a guidance system, and especially on the role of decision intelligence. Now we find even more deep-seated, subtle and diffuse features in technological society that must be addressed if society is to be the keeper of its technology.

People and Personhood

It is not agreeable to this author to treat the situation as though the world were distinguished only by political or institutional considerations and by abstract processes of social interaction. The world of our concern is one of people, indeed of individuals. A scholarly treatment of the psychological–spiritual dimensions of the subject at hand is beyond the competence of the author. Yet, to neglect concern for this most important character in the drama would be a serious flaw. Many critics of treatises like "Limits to Growth" point to its omission of a political framework. Although the political factor has been dealt with here, it would be equally culpable to fail to explore individual drives, aspirations, and behavior with respect to the future.

We now state explicitly several assumptions which up to this point have simply been implicit in this study. First, wide diversity among individuals must be expected, even treasured—diversity in spiritual depth, in emotional expression and intellectual horsepower, in interests, in energy, in sense of community and of compassion, and in dreams. Second, there is enormous potential in each person for growth, learning, self-realization and for spiritual achievement. Indeed, such maturity is essential to overcome excessive aggression and socially destructive drives. Society sets the game rules for acceptable behavior, by rewards and penalties. When challenged, most people respond with purposeful commitment. Moreover, each individual has hopes of living a family life of dignity and self-esteem within a humane society.

Despite the well-documented basic drive toward self-preservation, humankind is linked by a mysterious common bond of creative, selfless love. Many display spontaneous altruism that sociobiologists currently interpret as a genetic manifestation of action for survival of the species.

If this sounds baldly humanist, it must be admitted instantly that the humanist tradition, if not practice, has proved a fragile barrier against political bestiality; that modern education has not developed personal character so that the lapse from ceremony and ritual has left a serious vacuum; that urban life and mobility have dissolved community and kinship with resulting loss in individual identity; that the counter-culture has engaged in demolition of armchair habits without fulfilling a *noblesse oblige* of asserting new moral standards for personhood.

A number of social analysts conclude their vision of the future in a pessimistic vein because of ultimate limits they believe to be imposed by human nature. Aldous Huxley, Sir Charles Darwin, Robert Heilbroner see through the mists a continuation of hopeless exploitation and enslavement of one individual by another, of tribalism and blind acceptance of authority.[87] Others, while perceiving limits, consider them as pliable; they suggest retooling and regenerating the individual rather than institutions. The second approach is essential to this thesis. The time scale of concern here is over the next 75 years. In light of the progress humankind has made over the last 10,000 years, albeit fitfully, three-fourths of a century seems too short an interval to exhaust hope for human potential. On the other hand, with whatever genetic inheritance the human race exhibits collectively, even given the desire to alter human behavior, 75 years also seems too short an interval to accomplish basic and universal modification. Indeed, Sir Charles Darwin takes the view that even in a time scale of one million years human nature is immutable. So we must live with people the way they are.

There is, of course, an alternative: dealing with the crucial role of culture in human behavior. The cultural influence is known to be both changing and changeable. Some cultural discontinuities now seem to occur in as short as 20 years, although those in less than 50 seem accompanied by social indigestion and intergenerational conflicts. The socialization of the individual is of interest to us because a substantial fraction of survival skills are passed on by endowments of one generation to future generations in the form of culture and tradition, religion and law. These are then enriched by experience and education throughout a lifetime. But now, we are at an interval of human history where, as Margaret Mead put it, "nowhere in the world are there elders who know what the children know."[88] The stimuli from outside the family far exceed those passed on within.

So not only are survival skills not systematically indoctrinated; other cultural changes may have dulled even those passed on. Increased material abundance coupled with transfers of personal responsibility to government have reduced preparation of individuals for coping with transcendent perils. The new species of menace finds no one adequately prepared.

The instinct for survival and for security is surely as pronounced as ever. Its achievement no longer depends on solitary aggressiveness. Rather, it depends increasingly on new social learning for synergistic social activity. The individual living in a community has reason to look to a government to provide minimal conditions of existence. Paradoxically, with all of the abundance wrought by economic capitalism and technology, we do not have that minimum, either at a personal level of protection against street crime and violence or at a community level against nuclear war.

Moreover, there is ample evidence that whatever passes for civilization does not guarantee this protection to many individuals on the planet. Mass murder under Hitler is only one generation past, and its continuation, embroidered by excesses of brutality and torture, is widespread, episodic and by no means under control.

Our Western society places a high premium on personal liberty and opportunities for self-realization, creativity and diversity. One gets uneasy as to how firm this dedication may be, even in America. Platt's allusion to "Friendly Fascism" is but one observer's view that a nonviolent increase in levels of coercion might be tolerated as the majority of individuals choose to trade off liberty for promise of other pleasures, for satisfaction of every sensory appetite.[89] As one observer noted, humanism may not have the psychic leverage to meet that challenge.[90]

The basic absurdity of our time is that the economic system that was widely hailed as a technique for meeting all of the individual's basic needs increasingly requires pump priming, with consumption artfully stimulated by way of advertising. Spending for fashion rather than need did lead to economic growth whose surpluses fostered opportunities for education and leisure. But spending also led to wasting, exhausting, polluting and a condition of no leisure or too much. Instead of feeling gratified, more and more people seem unhappy, "united only by a sense of shared misfortune, depression and impotence."[91] Fundamentally, it is not high economic efficiency but high survivability that must characterize human civilization.

The relevance to this essay of such trends lies in the apparent shift of sentiment from classical notions of thrift, self-denial, sacrifice—all of which carried prospects of longer term benefits—to notions of immediate satisfaction of self-interest. To be sure, the Christian ethic helped charge the spiritual inclination to look ahead, to salvation. But today, as that pronounced cultural trait seems to evaporate and people think less of providing for the future, it is difficult to expect political leadership to preach more self-restraint.

Cultural trends toward mindless consumption are reinforced by faith in economic criteria of value, and in industrial techno-structures of our society catering to a fiction of paradise through material prosperity. Technical artifacts pump that trend faster. Aids exist for instant gratification, the "turn-on" of mechanical stimulation. The throb of music seems, as Steiner put it, to serve the young as a universal buffer or narcotic against boredom.

In a state of alienation, there seems to be an itch for crisis, or at least news of crisis elsewhere, and again the modern media serve up a scratching of global strife and calamity. Consider the following lead sentences in a national news magazine.[92] "Jimmy Carter was in the midst of a deepening crisis of confidence with businessmen—and, to a growing extent, with the public. . . ." "The stock market reacted to all these uncertainties in predictable fashion: it sank." "One of the touchiest problems inherited by the Carter Administration was the case of former CIA Director Richard M. Helms." "When the two-year drought first parched much of the country in 1976, farmers cried that unless Washington came to their rescue they faced financial ruin." "As expected, the U.N. Security Council voted 15 to 0 last week to impose a mandatory arms embargo on South Africa. . . ." "Advocates of recombinant DNA research have been insisting that potential benefits from the ingenious new technique of genetic engineering far outweigh any dangers that it could pose." "Medford High: Strife in the Suburbs."

There is both irony and tragedy in a civilization which, like Prometheus, has stolen fire from heaven but which yet lacks the insight, vision and moral commitment to resist the technological caress. Understandably, philosophers are crying out for spiritual rejuvenation as an antidote, and this author does not evade the issue.

With our primary focus on policy, the point of concern here is that a powerful connection exists between cultural values and political behavior, so that if there are potentially lethal consequences of political neglect of the future, they relate to the cultural myopia.

It will take more than a smidgen of political courage to move against these cultural tides in an era without a cause. Yet, given the diversity of human perspective mentioned earlier, a sizable fraction of the population should be interested and willing to join a charge to new heights of human progress. Such advances would be strengthened if more citizens had both a common appreciation of our modern dilemmas and opportunities to translate their views into action. How, then, do we counteract obstructions and hidden impediments to social achievement?

CHAPTER 7

New Scarcities

Scarcity of Time

Whatever we might do to mitigate obsession with the short run inevitably runs up against constraints of scarcities. One of these is the unremitting escapement of time.

How people view time is a subtle ingredient of culture, sometimes treated metaphysically but not often systematically. A graphic parody of Western culture was a New Yorker cartoon showing in successive blocks a man racing for his commuter train, then running from train to subway station, then rushing up the steps at his stop to find a bench in Central Park, open the morning paper—and read. Rushing is characteristic. So is the glamorization of speed. Performance is advertised in miles per hour, assembly line cars per day, new houses per year. In the pages of sexually oriented books and magazines, the number of experiences seems more important than their quality.

It is also clear that we still do not have time for certain basic activities: time to contemplate, to speculate and to think. Imaging the future requires all three.

This apparent scarcity of time is reflected in behavior. Because there is not enough time, what is available does double duty. As Russell says, everything is being done for the sake of something else rather than for its own sake.[(93)] Walter Kerr picks up this theme in observing that we "read for profit, party for contacts, lunch for contracts, bowl for unity, gamble for charity, go out in the evening for the greater glory of the municipality, and stay at home for the weekend to rebuild the house.—Isn't it odd that a century which should, by all rights, be the most leisurely in history is also known to be, and condemned for being, the fastest."[(94)] As Linder argued in his compelling and felicitous book, we have a "harried leisure class."[(95)]

Although we seldom recognize it this way, time is a resource. Ben Franklin's adage that time is money quickly sparks recall of personal experiences with that trade-off—in making home repairs rather than calling in a service man, or in paying overtime wages to get a job finished sooner, or in saving money by taking the time to shop wisely. When driving swiftly on dangerous roads, we trade off time and personal risk. We also trade off time and energy. Because energy is the rate of doing work, we can live with a much lower horsepower auto if we accept the delay penalty of climbing hills slowly. Most applied research has deadlines which require trade-offs of promptness for thoroughness.

In politics, time may be traded off for power. Seeking consensus may require patient teaching or bargaining, without which a key debate may be lost. The compression of time, like the compression of a gas, is likely to be accompanied by an increase in temperature. In a conflict situation, compromise may fail without time for cooling off.

When discussing stress in the decision theater, we pointed out that fundamental pathologies in response differed significantly on the perception of time—too much or too little. In one case there was pathological delay; in another panic.

Congress points with pride at the number of bills it introduces each session, the number debated and enacted. Seldom is there concern with whether the time invested in study is consistent with virility of estimated consequences. Seldom does the leadership examine and give precedence to legislation on the basis of a rationale corresponding to the schedule of threats outlined earlier.

Almost universally, policy makers complain about there being too little time to study alternatives; yet they would agree that mulling over issues is an essential adjunct to good judgment. Thus, bureaucratic footdragging that was twitted earlier may have its virtues. Nevertheless, politicians become vague as to what the pacing element may be. Sometimes, as in a genuine crisis, the barn door must be closed swiftly to cut losses. But as often as not, the clock is considered running only because of an imagined loss in opportunity. In political competition, an advocate's delay almost always seems to accrue to someone else's advantage. Thus, jockeying for political advantage may often be the main hurry.

Few in the political arena break that pattern, or realistically should be expected to.

To engage this dilemma posed by the clock, we are obliged to ask how the scarcity of time undermines the decision theater and how it increases probabilities of error. First, decision making takes time—to sort out goals, search for and process information bearing on the issue, to generate options and to trace consequences. Some degree of uncertainty inevitably prevails, and this can be somewhat mitigated by gathering more information, but at a price—taking time. As the consequences of oversight or error become more serious, such investments of time are all the more warranted. But the parade of issues with increasing technical complexity, social interconnectedness and technology-induced options makes the information processing more and more costly, and to the policy maker must be weighed against a daily agenda of other imperatives in a hectic atmosphere. The number of choices is not declining, and less and less time rather than more time is devoted on the average to each decision. Without adequate study in this competition for attention, the quality of decisions suffers. Something occurs like impulse buying of advertisement-stimulated consumer appetites. Consideration of the long term is squeezed out.

The element of time affects contemporary decision processes in yet one other, subtle way because of growing complexity in social process. Given the number and diversity of actors in a technological delivery system and differentiation in their goals, their interlocking activities need to be synchronized. Yet, each is likely to sense an issue at different times and proceed at different rates to engage it fully. As the number of participants increases, more time is needed to interact.

Most scholars in the field also agree that the pace of crisis-induced action may now exceed the natural rhythm and time horizons of human experience, and certainly the rate at which institutions can adjust. On the other hand, if that system response were in phase with stimuli, it might be so swift as to lose the predictability essential for smooth functioning. The velocity of knowledge generation is not matched by social assimilation.

Herbert A. Simon views time in the decision process another way.[96] Since information is not gratis, it must be acquired in a time-constrained search. And since the examination of alternatives and consequences is likely to be incomplete, the *sequence* in which impacts are examined becomes highly influential in choice. If policy makers do examine impacts in the sequence outlined earlier in Table 2, and for want of adequate time trace through only the initial half of the list, virtually none of the factors bearing on the health of the decision process, much less on longer-incubating impacts, will get any play.

In terms of decision malfunctions touched upon earlier, time compression would increase susceptibility to loss in steering capacity and coordination. Swift impulses generate overreaction to crisis followed by the backlash of excessive feedback. From lessons taught by engineering, we learned that gradually applying loads to a beam or increasing damping reduces overshoot. Also, recalling the automobile analogy, risk is increased if visibility is obscured and road signs are passed in swift succession as to be unintelligible. Safe drivers slow down.

So while the need to think through important social consequences multiplies, the time between choices shrinks. Stress increases. The quality of choice is adversely affected, especially in neglecting the future, and gradually the decision apparatus is itself undermined.

Whatever the literature reports as a new era of scarcity of resources, of energy, and of funds to do all we wish, we have an even more excruciating shortage of time.

Since time cannot be stockpiled, what can we do? For one thing we could take more time. Taking more time may involve trade-offs so as to allot more to one deliberation at the expense of another. Alternatively, taking more time may mean slowing down. That is a violently heretical notion in an era of political turbulence over a wide range of issues. But slowing down the decision process has no direct connection to velocities of social achievement. Indeed, a slower but wiser choice in social strategy may in the long run be advantageous, to reduce risk, cost, waste of resources and sources of stress. But this is based on the assumption that the extra time would be invested in policy-relevant research, diffusion of hard facts and implications for common understanding and conflict resolution, a quenching rather than stimulation of adversarial attitudes.

Political actors as well as citizens may need new garments of self-control, and there are numerous ways the rules of the game could be modified without inequitable political penalty.

If citizens clamor for better decisions in terms of outcomes rather than decision speed, and if the political reward system signals that preference, change could be induced in top-level decision behavior.

Here, we run up against the barrier of our culture. Linder makes a compelling point that a lifeway dominated by the clock is in part a consequence of our addiction to economic growth and to consumer goods. With that distortion of a means to an end in itself, the yield on time increases so as economically to make it scarce. More than that, our affluence takes the form only of access to goods, and since it takes time to enjoy or consume them, time in our society becomes scarce and becomes the ultimate limit to consumption. But then, there is no leisure, no slack for contemplation or for citizen participation, or even much lighthearted play. In contrast, economically poor cultures have a surplus of time. In some, there is a distinguished practice of thoughtful decision-making that is mindful of tragic consequences of error.

Habits are formed by everyone, citizen and policy maker, in their daily lives of having to make more frequent decisions with less study for each. These patterns are bound to be projected from the micro-decision to the macro-decision theater. Presidents, goaded by the press, take pride in what they can accomplish in the first hundred days, because people expect speed.

Changes in these cultural patterns are said by anthropologists to require at least 20 years. If a start were made now, could the suggested improvements be made in time to meet the dilemmas marching toward us? Except for a few, the prospects are encouraging. It is those few particular threats to survival therefore that deserve priority policy attention because of the lethal consequences of neglect. A slowdown in policy areas related to survival might have two favorable results. First, some investments might be made for improvement of the total decision system that have broad portents to meet the problems ahead. And the decisions then made are likely to produce more socially satisfactory outcomes.

At stake is a balance among considerations of the past, the present and the future. Professor Harold A. Linstone in an unpublished analysis of the situation puts it this way. Primary focus on the past is oriented by feeling, largely toward sentimental attachment to continuity of historic trends. Primary focus on the present is oriented by crisis that requires instant relief regardless of future cost; and exclusive focus on the future becomes speculative, utopian and normative, a form of dreaming but vulnerable to loss in contact with reality. Only by an effective synthesis of all three time frames can we integrate three basic human qualities of intellect, emotion and spirit that underpin survival.

Scarcity of Activists

Only a prompt and radical change in behavior can liberate us from a dominant concern for the short run. How will such resolute activism occur, and who will lead it?

To readers who regard themselves as devout practitioners of liberal politics and citizen participation, the notion that activists are in short supply is likely to be an anathema. At first glance, the procession of movements and of social change after World War II would seem to contradict the proposition of scarcity.

Volunteer groups such as the Commission to Study the Organization of Peace helped implant a perspective that all peoples on the planet have common interests in survival with self-esteem, and thus the institutional need for a United Nations. Peace movements were ignited in a vivacious counterpoise to the bland administration of President Eisenhower. Americans for Democratic Action took initiatives in numerous social causes. Hubert Humphrey exemplified the role of courageous activist in the U.S. Congress. President Kennedy began to lead the Executive Branch attack on economic, social and racial inequality. President Lyndon B. Johnson sought to advance the charge until bogged down by Viet Nam.

By the late 1960s, the hot passions aroused by that nonwar boiled over into intense social turbulence. So did the smouldering racial issues that flamed in Watts and soon literally ignited fires in many American cities. But other emotional attacks on broader social questions were diffuse and strikingly deficient in a coherent and reasoned program. Citizen activism all too often dealt with symptoms, not with causes. And activism has often been an attempt to break out of feelings of powerlessness and futility; the substantive thrust is simply a vehicle.

Among the devils to be exorcised by the counterculture were technology and the political–military–industrial–scientific complex. The neo-Luddite anti-technology movement reflected a basic fear, as much for being left out of political process as for the concerns expressed over dehumanization.

Some movements, however, gained purchase on the questions through effective use of facts and analysis. Ralph Nader took on the issue of technological malfeasance by publicizing unsafe performance of the Corvair. Through several national organs such as Public Citizen and a covey of regional Public Interest Research Groups, Nader tapped a reservoir of underutilized intellectual talent of dedicated citizens. Additionally, a small band of effective activists dealt with the environment where the establishment was conspicuously vulnerable. The cross-Florida barge canal was stopped. The Trans-Alaska Pipeline was forced to be reengineered.[97]

The common ingredient of these targets was credible imminence of the threat. Almost completely lacking was an activist position dealing with the longer run, less certain but more virulent dangers.

A reviewer of a book describing public interest science initiatives picks up the point that while such groups have alleviated some existing "technological Viet Nams," they do little about preventing future errors. One of the reasons is that there is "little analysis as to why the system gets out of joint," simply a tendency to paint the establishment as a "confused, corrupted monolith," still awaiting an examination as to why it so behaves and where the responsibility lies.[98]

In the 1960s, voices of revolution on the college campus, while sometimes shrill, were influential in prodding a cultural shift, but they have been quiet since the Viet Nam excursion ended. Even the voices for arms control seem largely exhausted. The primary exception has been citizen concern about harmful effects of nuclear power, but even here, several state referenda in 1976 to stop new construction until safety was better assured failed.

Citizen activism in 1978 seems transformed to single-issue politics, with innumerable lobbyists zealously vying for public as well as political attention. The resulting noise level not only distracts attention from the overarching issues; it may dissolve the limited energies of those who want to fasten on them.

The role of activism to deal with the future is not exclusively that of citizen movements. There is the White House itself. Earlier, the

President was singled out as the nation's systems manager. The incumbent occupies the central position of power to sense and set national priorities of public purpose and public purse, to harness the psychic energies of a variegated people with a delicate balance among interest groups. Given that members of Congress are obliged to consider their geographically local or functionally parochial supporters, only the President has a universal constituency. This does not shield him from intense and varied pressures, requirements for compromise, bargaining and accommodation, or sensitivity to rugged constraints of law and of resources. And it does not isolate him either from trade-offs between the long and short term.

Of all the political actors and activists, the President has the greatest opportunity to deal with issues of the future.

This raises questions of his resources to do so and his disposition. Action by President Jimmy Carter on energy conservation in the United States furnished a concrete test, and the track record satisfied no one.

On the matter of resources to deal with the future, the President has access to the entire Executive Branch. Of particular interest, however, is the Office of Science and Technology Policy, created by the National Science and Technology Policy, Organization and Priorities Act, PL 94-282. Signed into law May 11, 1976, this measure restored a technology-related staff function that had been created by President Eisenhower as an Office of Special Assistant to the President for Science and Technology in November 1957. Chronicled elsewhere is the story of its triggering by the Soviet space surprise, its early effectiveness in counseling on military security issues, its legislative underpinning in 1962 to afford Congress better access, its role as advocate for science funding. But by 1966 it was wallowing in civilian-related issues, eventually lost its effectiveness, and in a final collision with its boss, was dismantled by President Nixon in June 1973.(99)

Subsequently, Congress sought to reestablish this function, based on at least four different rationales. The scientific community argued that issues before the President were increasingly sophisticated and needed independent in-house technical expertise, thus supporting resuscitation of the earlier function.(100) Other testimony averred that the specific office should not be rebuilt, but that instead a modified function was needed for the public management of technology-related governmental policy,[101] including a better balance of staff with social as well as natural science expertise.[102] Special emphasis was placed by the American Society for Public Administration on OSTP's role to coordinate federal agencies and on reciprocal communication with state and local governments which were increasingly expected to implement programs for which their diversity of views was needed in advance of federal decisions.[103] Fourth, there was a faint but unmistakable advocacy that the new office constitute an early warning function for the President.[104]

It is the fourth argument that interests us here. In the language of the Act, Section 101(a) opens with the panegyric: "The Congress, recognizing the profound impact of science and technology on society . . .", finds in subsection 2 that factors which "influence the course of national and international events require appropriate provision, involving long-range, inclusive planning. . . ." Section 101(a)6 states that "the Nation's capabilities for technology assessment and for technological planning and policy formulation must be strengthened at both Federal and State levels."

The declaration of policy asserts principles in Section 102(a)1 that strategies should be based on "a continuous appraisal of the role of science and technology in achieving goals and formulating policies. . . ." Section 5 calls for "strong participation and cooperative relationships with State and local governments" and "increased public understanding of science and technology."

On implementation, the Act asserts that central policy planning elements should be maintained to anticipate "future concerns to which science and technology can contribute . . ."; and as to procedures, Section 102(c)2 states that "Particular attention should be given to . . . problems and opportunities that are so long-range, geographically widespread or economically diffused that the Federal Government constitutes the appropriate source for undertaking their support."

Title II established the OSTP in the Executive Office of the President, and assigned it tasks in Section 205(a) to "initiate studies and analyses, including systems analyses and technology assessments, of alternatives available for the resolution of critical and emerging national and international problems . . .", and in subsection 10, to "identify and assess emerging and future areas in which science and technology can be effectively used. . . ."

On looking ahead, Section 206(a) calls for the preparation of a five-year outlook on current and emerging problems. Section 209(a) calls for an annual report that, among other contents, shall "discuss significant effects of current and projected trends in science and technology on social, economic and other requirements of the nation," and a "forecast of critical and emerging national problems the resolution of which . . ." involves technology.

A President's Committee on Science and Technology of outsiders, called for in Title III, Section 303(a), is asked to prepare a survey focused among other things on "(3) improved technology assessment in the Executive Branch of the Federal Government."

Whatever such legislation may authorize as to a presidential staff arm, implementation depends entirely on the incumbent President's style, wishes and instructions. He can ask for more, or for much less. In the early childhood of any agency such as OSTP, a competition for power is bound to erupt, especially in gaining the ear of the President. Older units in the Executive Office inevitably claim that all of the intended functions are already being carried out so that any new unit is redundant. They are sure to impede its growth whenever possible.

Dealing with the long run issues, however, has seldom been on the agenda of such presidential staff agencies, themselves conditioned to crisis and its management. One experimental ad hoc effort assigned by President Nixon in 1970 to Patrick Moynihan was abruptly terminated, but not before a candid and visionary report was released, focusing among other matters on the role of technology assessment.[105]

The politician as activist has an opportunity to break out of the mold of merely synthesizing what voters want. Instead, he can assert what people ought to think about, ought to want, and ought to have. He can criticize trends and illumine alternatives.

With the renaissance of the OSTP, an opportunity clearly existed for the President to employ this new advisory enterprise in anticipatory analysis.

By November 1977, President Carter's intentions regarding OSTP were clear. Staff allocations were so limited as to be symbolic rather than functional. A federal council to coordinate the bureaucracy and an advisory committee to extend OSTP capabilities were essentially killed. By late 1978, no early warning function was evident. OSTP seemed destined to be a limited reincarnation of its predecessor.

As the President engages more and more technology-laden problems, and as difficulties grow in matching them by effective policy remedies, all may prove intransigent. Every policy initiative may extract enormous political energy until a new appraisal is made of the decision process itself and its disabilities. Then, an activist President might tackle the most demanding task of all—dealing with underlying pathologies of the short run.

Not only on specific issues, but on the overarching issues of collective security, the vital role of an activist President is to reach out to the citizenry, to waken them to an understanding of the precarious situation and of every individual's responsibility to endow the future. This can be done only be weighing future needs against short term wants.

Scarcity of Reserves

Earlier, we contrasted military with nonmilitary threat situations, both as to the disposition to look ahead and the availability of resources for vigilance and contingencies. The latter issue is one of liquidity. For whatever reason in civilian activities, the economic surpluses promised by technological leverage seem paradoxically to have been exhausted if not overcommitted, and this shortfall induces a fundamental problem in a society so characterized by change. One cause of scarcity in resources is that unplanned correctives are repeatedly called upon with short notice to deal with unwanted effects of, and waste associated with, past myopic decisions. Opportunistic incrementalism that characterizes modern decision making ultimately exacts its toll. Another major factor in the absence of liquidity is the project approach of technology. Technological delivery systems are organized around narrow goals that are attacked so vigorously that the collective demand for resources always exceeds the supply. The result is to soak up all available resources, even to mortgage the future.

The very act of change in direction or in speed requires energy. Some small yet finite amount is required in the guidance system; even more for implementation. Complexity and interconnectedness also soak up resources because transaction costs for collaboration are increased. Unless deliberate allocations are made for decision analysis, future shifts will become less and less graceful. As all parties in the system sense the lack of reserves to meet emergencies, even motivation to vigilance is undermined.

Additional resources are also necessary for learning. As the past has become less and less a guide for the future, dealing with novelty imposes demands for new knowledge that cannot be met if all intellectual resources are fully committed. Research and development constitutes one such learning activity, especially vital when the political apparatus stands in need of new information to meet impending problems. Yet, the process of funding R & D has itself become so laborious and obsessed with politically "safe" projects to head off congressional ridicule that the start of any new study is delayed until years after conception, with little slack in project funding to pick up new and promising trends of thought or react to sudden policy requirements. Moreover, there is a similar lack of disposition to look at effectiveness of the R & D decision process itself.

Most serious, however, is the extremely limited capability for early warning and forecasting, for phrasing of alternative responses and tracing consequences of each.

Industry and commerce well understand constraints that are imposed without liquidity in funds. New opportunities are lost, and reserves are too weak to meet the unexpected. Business practices constantly monitor availability of such contingency funds. Individuals do the same with personal savings.

Government, almost alone, seems dangerously unaware of the need to prepare for a rainy day. In engineering parlance, preparedness is couched in terms of safety margins, and in titling this book we have utilized the same concept in the phrase *margins for survival*.

CHAPTER 8

Strategies of Technological Choice: New Social Learning for Collective Security

Appreciating the Situation: A Cultural Stance

This inquiry opened with the question as to why the policy apparatus is deaf to signals of the future—warnings of threats to survival from a battery of global dangers. Many answers have been uncovered.

To approach the critical task of devising strategies for collective security, we first reflect on a broad social posture that must bolster explicit proposals to follow. To be sure, given the sweep of this undertaking and the thicket of technical, political and psychological processes involved, it has been difficult to do justice to all fundamental issues involved. Sorting out "what's the problem" has been conspicuously brief. Details have been omitted; comprehensive documentation has been short-circuited; interpretation has been simplified; use of intricate social science methodology has been suppressed. Yet a composite panorama emerges.

The past has become less and less a guide for the future. Especially where cause–effect processes evaporate as aids to navigation, we become more dependent on the social equivalent of dead reckoning. At the same time, the health of the decision process is jeopardized. Then we become more vulnerable to serious lapses in judgment, human error and just plain ignorance in trying to survive.

Many explorers of the future have glimpsed this same condition and the urgency of new social strategies for collective security. Some have recoiled in gloom. Roberto Vacca believes the technological delivery system is so technically complex as to be beyond human control.[(106)] Rufus E. Miles concludes that the same system is so politically and socially complex as to transcend limits of human management.[(107)] Jay

Forrester contends that the major forces at work are almost deterministic and insensitive to policy guidance.[108] Robert Heilbroner argues that the limits to human character predispose the future to a fatalistic, unceasing and irreversible decline.[109]

Yet, to do nothing, to hope to muddle through, is capitulation to blind fate, an admission that we can make no sense from what is happening. "The consequent triumph of ignorance," predicts Brzezinski, "extracts its own tribute in the form of unstable and reactive policies."[110]

The most hopeful contemporary philosophers do make it clear that we are at a crossroads. Our paradigm must be shifted, perhaps as Schumaker suggests, to small being beautiful.[111] Or, as Teilhard de Chardin and Reich propose, to patterns of feeling and of spirituality.[112] Renewing ourselves is a virtue in its own right, but the track record of sustained voluntary behavioral reform is not convincing. Fear of the devil has generally evaporated.

Even the notion of retooling our major institutions does not stir the blood, especially where institutions are so palpably resistant to new ideas that may rock the status quo of comfortable accommodation. And few in our society are willing to give organizations even greater precedence over people. Indeed, there is a basic question as to whether society is in a state of readiness to change, and if so, to what?

A basic premise on which to begin was poignantly stated fifty years ago by Alfred North Whitehead, "It is the business of the future to be dangerous." Interpreting that stark reality, Kenneth Boulding contends that the fundamental condition of the 20th century is that we live precariously in the midst of a great transition, where a livable and enduring society will require commitment of human energy, resources and enlightenment exceeding that of all precursors.[113] As viewed by John Platt, any such social change must be powered by "what might be."[114]

Yet, we seem to have exhausted our capacity to image that future, perhaps even to image reality. To the extent that vision exists, its extreme variations and associated cognitive dissonance reveal what Vickers deems the absence of appreciating the situation, a "shared system of interpretation to enable humans to influence one another."[115] This missing foundation is nowhere more dangerous than in the general absence of images of those futures people do *not* want.

The problems are not, as many social critics contend, that we are suffering from the wake of a technological imperative, but rather from deficiencies in political and intellectual institutions in foreseeing consequences of no action or the wrong action. Solutions must thus be sought primarily in cultural, institutional and political change, not in technical.

The quandary being far from simple, we must expect a strategy for survival to be equally complex. We are obliged to examine and to consider for remedial action not only the organizational components of the technological delivery system, especially in government, but also the dynamic processes involved. The cognitive map set forth earlier pictured this web of social activities and their interactions.

In the first instance, political action generally reflects the collective will of what people want. As it relates to improved balance between long run and short run benefits, will people defer gratification? Will they make the necessary sacrifices? Or will chronic anxiety about the unknown increase susceptibility to quick and popular nostrums, or worse, to a yearning for order that is promised by tyrants? And can traditional institutions better integrate technical opportunities with social preferences that will be mindful of longer range impacts?

We find that dispositions to the short run are deeply engraved in the cultural setting, yet that is the salient area to be dealt with, and its modification the most difficult.

Basic biological needs and instinctive drives for survival find ultimate expression in these cultural values and socialization practices. For millennia such patterns were transmitted from generation to generation as the most powerful symbolic templates or blueprints for the organization of both collective social and individual psychological processes. But now the past fails as a teacher.

Given that survival of the species is the transcendent goal, we may need a new survival kit in collective learning and action. In a free society, this requires consensus, underscoring again the criticality of a shared cultural stance based on factual knowledge and understanding, on estimates of threat and on mutuality of expectations. To be sure, modern diversity, which is widely admired, carries with it a cultural eclecticism that challenges collective decisions. Nevertheless, survival of a humanistic democratic society basically depends on large numbers of people making thoughtful, realistic choices, with the aid of appropriate information.

Thomas Jefferson, who was a clarion advocate of civic education, tutored the nation with the epigram that "people cannot be safe without information."

The problem is not just information for managing complexity and the growing pains of a large social system, but keeping it within bounds of citizen comprehension.[116] The learning curve for our society seems to be lagging requirements for citizenship. But since learning is presumptive for an individual, it is also possible for a people. There is even a possibility that people may learn faster than institutions. So that national politics may be freed both from the stigma of a charade, as some observers call it,[117] and from the malady of deafness to signals of the future, there must somehow be established an agreement that the steering of technology in such a way that we may survive with self-esteem is largely a political act, and that citizens, rather than politicians alone, should write the script.

A shared cultural stance based on common information brings to mind that social systems are communications networks. The commodity of exchange is knowledge and information. Yet, it is a shocking paradox that with the present exponential growth of technical knowledge, people know so little about what is going on or what perils may lie ahead. Not only is technical knowledge generated by a small group of scientists and engineers, it is interpreted and applied by a similar cadre. Here we encounter serious problems in diffusion and common understanding. The problem is not one of deficiency in specialized knowledge. The condition of ignorance arises from the absence of shared data and translation for wider understanding.

For one thing, we have entered an era where knowledge is treated as private property, impounded by government, protected by patent and copyright, and cordoned off by proprietary corporate fences. Even in academia, tendencies are widely recognized to establish disciplinary boxes protected by primitive territorialism.

Attempts at interdisciplinary communication are generally undernourished, undermined and even punished. Paradigms or rigid patterns of thought become ennobled, challenging a few rebels to break through the structure of scientific evolution and to joust with adherents to taxonomy and method.[118] Seldom in the knowledge generation function is there a sense of broader pattern, a problem rather than discipline orientation to research, or a commitment to foster public understanding of science and technology. The "citadel of expertise" sometimes arrogantly requests support with public funds without a corresponding responsibility of interpreting social implications for the citizen as sponsor.

In raising the question of sensitivity to today's overarching perils, we must admit that each has received only meager public recognition and symbolic governmental study. And nowhere has there been a holistic overview. We deal with one thing at a time, piecemeal and in response to crisis. Policies are reactive rather than anticipatory.

The point here is that a basic deficiency in policy to deal with the future lies in a flabbiness of citizen interest in the future and indifference to the fact that bills for today's decision to meet only the short run are sure to come due tomorrow.

Clearly, a better forum is required for development and exchange of ideas and general perceptions, instead of mere response to the jerk of events. The objective is not simply greater effectiveness in problem solving, but deeper understanding of the problem setting.[119] Scientific facts should be mixed with social judgments. By such common understanding, institutions as well as individuals are better prepared to deal with complexity and interdependence on a day-to-day basis, and to sense the future in terms of consequences of today's decisions or their default. As was said before, coherence among the separate players is built with public policy.

Policy decisions at the top will include a balanced consideration of the future only if political pressures to do so are sufficiently intense and continuous, and political acts rewarded. Informed public participation is the gist of a deep-rooted appreciation of the future. It is strongest when it springs from a grass roots creed.

Such a creed could be nurtured by general education for citizenship that includes a greater sense of how the system works, of citizen responsibility to foster wise political choice, and of the powerful realities of future impact.

Such energy has been evoked locally when threats were personalized; a variety of public interest organizations has issued report cards on incumbent congressmen and believes that such monitoring and publicity have influenced the outcome of elections.

At some point, the breadth and depth of public concern for the future becomes a movement. This has been the rationale of Common Cause. John Platt contemplates a movement for world survival.[120] By legitimate intervention in decision making it could balance the political forces and bureaucratic inertia that tend to the short run by making the social cost too high to neglect future consequences of present decisions. Enhanced grass roots comprehension and involvement could also reduce oppressiveness of excessive centralization, the technical parochialism and social isolation associated with decision making by the bureaucracy, the elite and the expert.

Now we begin to see a second connection between the roots of culture and the towers of policy making. With better tools of information, creed of future concern and heightened involvement, citizens could be intimately involved in long range planning. Rather than simply assent to policy, the electorate could contribute to it. With bottom-up rather than top-down planning, there could be a "participatory technology."[121]

There have been some notable experiments in participatory planning, one in the State of Washington that provided instruction on potentialities, but then, with a shift in administration, failed in follow-through. In 1977, New Zealand established a Commission for the Future with a similar objective of coupling national policy making with a citizen choice as to the way ahead. It will be interesting to watch this development in contrast with Sweden's corresponding efforts through a high level Secretariat for Future Studies located in its Ministry for Foreign Affairs.[122] Gerlach and Hine[123] propose general techniques for this step from concepts of "networks engaged in participatory futurization."

For people to participate, however, they have to want a future. Most, but by no means all, do hope for celestial qualities of human opportunity as described previously. But unless they have encouragement, education, explicit images of the future they may *not* want, together with mechanisms to deepen their understanding and engage their energies in political action, fantasy will not translate to reality.

Survival Training: Education for the Future

Education along with the mass media is a principal social means for influencing the basic core of a national culture. Whatever the strengths or weaknesses of modern higher education, it is almost universally agreed that years in school are no guarantee of a greater sense of virtue, a higher social wisdom or a more prescient insight of political manipulation. Formal excellence does not correlate with better social decision making, singly or in groups. Indeed, there is little that passes for civic education simply in terms of preparation for the responsibility of citizenship and, in order to preserve political freedom, for distinguishing true from false. Except for a symbolic act in professional schools, there is little concern for teaching of ethics. Gordon Rattray Taylor put his finger on this problem[(124)] when he said: "We need to teach young people about the social contract, the nature of democracy and about ethics . . . the moral pros and cons of change." Character training has been traditionally left to family and church, and the precepts of personal responsibility, self-sacrifice, deferred indulgence and morality have been heaved overboard by many young people determined to break with the past. As apparent in the scandals of cheating by students, ethics seems most visible in the breach.

That is not a dazzling report card.

In technological delivery systems, educational institutions were mapped as generators of new knowledge. They are significantly linked, however, to the technology policy apparatus and to the body politic. A set of educationally related issues is inevitably raised that bear on the main theme of orienting policy to the future:

—What new educational curricula and mechanisms are necessary to enrich citizen appreciation, generally?
—What curricula are essential to provide the younger generation with better survival kits?
—What reforms are indicated in scientific and engineering education and research?

Earlier it was observed that decision skills are largely self-taught; formal education on how to choose has generally been lacking or, where present in higher education, thinly spread and occasionally esoteric. The basic notion of John Dewey goes untended that the true purpose of knowledge lies in making choices among alternatives based on estimates of future consequences.[125]

Formal education to deal with the future is similarly neglected. History is seldom taught in terms of lessons for the way ahead. Processes of innovation and change are widely ignored, and only recently has there been a smattering of academic offerings with such titles as "Creating the Future" to dilate perspective. There is little guidance on how to manage risk and uncertainty, to cope in a technological society, individually or institutionally.

One major problem with higher education, except in professional schools, is its determined isolation from the real world. This practice not only renders the curriculum less and less relevant, it also delays entrance of young adults into the real world and inadvertently stretches adolescence and its associated narcissisms. The discipline-oriented structure of academic departments in no way coincides with the functions or problems of our society. In most academic institutions, few horizontal channels are open to compensate.

Impediments in universities to interdisciplinary problem-oriented programs include:

—difficulty in gaining high level institutional appreciation of the social situation and support for innovation;
—lack of rewards and freedom from penalties for faculty choosing this activity;
—failures in communication due to specialized jargon;
—lack of pedagogy and standards;
—resistance to experiential learning in addition to didactic;
—elaborate clearance procedures, to start new courses, for example;
—the need to build and tend bridges by bargaining with other campus units;
—meeting competitive tactics; and as a result,
—high transaction costs.

A second major problem is the technical illiteracy of many university graduates obliged to live in a technological world. Very few survey courses in natural sciences and engineering are taught for students not destined to enter these specialties. Moreover, on most campuses the sciences are segregated spatially as well as spiritually from each other and from the arts and humanities. With notable exceptions, engineering schools focus on technical artifacts and ignore society as clients, as well as the role of culture and social process in technological enterprise. And says one observer, "The absence of history of science and technology from the school syllabus is a scandal."[126]

A new agenda for the university will be required if we are to have an education for the future. The graduates of such education should be distinguished by breadth rather than specialization, schooled in a problem-centered rather than discipline-centered philosophy, versatile, adaptable, understanding of technologically induced processes of change, capable of self-discovery and self-expression, better able to distinguish truth, eager to participate in governance, able to make decisions and willing to assume self-discipline and personal responsibility for their fate.

And, as Toffler recalled, some of the most vital images of the future spring from education.[127]

The same challenge exists in continuing education for the citizen already out of school. There is almost a complete oversight of bonds between education and work, and these activities are treated as sequential rather than mutually reinforcing. Again, nourishment for citizenship is left to chance. In that vacuum, mass media become the major source of information and interpretation. Readers and electronic media consumers are seldom treated as thinking adults who might wish to undertake independent analysis. Universities could play some role in this development. Broad-band cable television has been widely suggested as the instrument for reaching people's consciousness in modes to which they are already addicted.

There are also two well-established instruments—the public library and the museum—that have had influential roles in education of the past. One serves as a collector and distributor of documents; the other as archivist and displayer of cultural artifacts. These roles could be revitalized. For example, the complexities and subtleties of science seem most effectively communicated to a layperson through graphic models, films or active demonstration. Here and there, museums portray key scientific concepts such that on repeated visits, citizens gain a basic comprehension of major discoveries and a feel as to how science works. One can also imagine a "museum of the future," displaying alternative ways ahead that are based on foreseeable consequences of current technical trends and opportunities, and different options before the nation.

Libraries could perform a related function by making available in readily comprehensible form the key political issues before the Congress or State Legislature, with a reference shelf of back-up material. Branch libraries throughout the country could be wired to the Congressional Research Service to tap the various data registers that already summarize legislatively relevant information for their representatives; this would extend proposals in the Congress to wire reference services in state capitols to CRS. Congressmen say they would like to have an informed electorate; they could consider aids to that process.

Finally, with suitable equipment, library clientele might "vote" on alternatives, register preferences and scan the evolving informal consensus. Interaction is even possible—a new mode of communication between government and the governed.

It would be tempting to elaborate on hardware for public participation. Other authors have detailed such opportunities, and the only comment to add is a cautionary note. A wired society makes political propaganda easier, and "engineered" consent is one of the subtle dangers catalogued earlier. That risk places survival of democracy through large numbers of people making realistic choice in the presence of adequate information directly against the arts of selling.[128]

This catalog of educational default is ironic in a science-based society, because science provides for all citizens one of the most salient philosophical telescopes for a cultural sighting on the future.

Science was termed by Vannever Bush as the endless frontier.[129] Indeed, it has a basic vector ahead, and it is intrinsically dynamic. It is the discoveries of science, translated by technology, that now pulse most changes in our society and trigger concerns about survival. The very conduct of science assumes progress in the sense that new knowledge unrelentingly modifies its precursors. Science is intrinsically in a constant state of revision, but because the processes are stable enough, it survives, even thrives, on change. Steiner explains C. P. Snow's dichotomy of two cultures as due to the fact that scientists look forward while humanists look backward.[130]

A second aspect is founding of the scientific edifice on observable and validated fact, not on doctrine. The ethos of science blooms from a devotion to truth as the most fundamental value. Facts take precedence over individual authority. Science also creates a formal network linking man and nature.

Science thus forms a root of our culture in both its substance and its process—the commitment to truth and the uncloaking of natural law to meet human needs. Yet science is isolated as an activity of the mind, and scientists are isolated in our culture as a proud subset of the intellectual elite.

To be sure, science and politics have had long associations, but these have been unsteady and often ambivalent.[131] In America, science has always sought and expected freedom from political interference. At the same time, research since World War II has been primarily sponsored by the federal government for reasons of military security; government is still a major client of results. Both parties have an abiding interest in that symbiotic relationship. For a substantial part of the 1957–1973 interval, when the President had a scientific advisor and staff, that White House unit guarded the health of science, using growth in federal R & D funding as a yardstick. The universities came to depend on that support and became understandably nervous whenever it wavered. Then, the scientific community began to lobby, with uneven success.

Slowly, uncritical support of science by both branches of Congress and the citizen has vanished, to some extent out of dismay over scientists advocating a *carte blanche* increase of 15 per cent per year.[132] Simultaneously, pique by President Johnson and anger by President Nixon were engendered because the Science Advisor's Office and its constituency refused to be used as political agents of the presidency. President Nixon then disestablished it altogether. Political significance of the still young OSTP is not clear.

Scientific fact nevertheless enters the brightly lit and noisy arena of political debate, increasingly over unwanted consequences, but without any deep understanding by the public of science or scientists.

Experts are often arrayed on both sides of an adversary proceeding. Facts are aften trotted out selectively, masquerading as unimpeachable. So questions for the layperson constantly arise as to what is authoritative, especially as it relates to the uncertain future. The cultural split remains unmended.

Whatever the basis for a raucous dichotomy between the academic and the citizen, it is a weakness in society's preparation for the future. The time may be ripe for a new coalition between the scientific community and the citizen.

Coalition Politics: New Collaboration between Scientists, Engineers and Citizens

To most readers, a new political coalition composed of scientists, engineers and citizens brings to mind two considerations—the general role of power blocs in moving the apparatus of government, influencing priorities and allocating resources, and the strengthening of influence of otherwise separate and weak pressure groups by their unity. For the moment, we shall skip these classical implications because they are self-evident, and instead explore the needs each partner in a scientist–citizen coalition has of the other, and the benefits to society of such federation.

That scientists and citizens are key, discrete elements in the technological delivery system becomes obvious as the first group is identified as knowledge producers associated with basic and applied research, and the second as the clients of technological output, in essence, the knowledge consumers. Connecting these polar extremities is the network of private and public institutions that utilize scientific discoveries, absorbing, selecting and applying technical knowledge in combination with physical and human resources to produce the goods and services that characterize a technological society. In that flow, very little direct intercourse occurs between the scientific community and the public.

The mediating institutions, incidentally, clearly understand that in their terms of reference knowledge is power. Both commercial establishments and individual agencies of government exploit new knowledge aggressively in terms of their separate and necessarily narrowly perceived goals. The scientific community as such has no control over the use or misuse of their contributions and, indeed, the very ethical distinction between benign or malignant consequences may not be their concern. On the other hand, the general public that has both a universal, if not justified, expectation as to the benefits of science and a collective social conscience as to applications is in the dark. For to them, science is inaccessible.

The chasm between scientist and citizen is pried open further by the public's confrontation with scientific complexity. Tedious efforts to understand are unfulfilled in an emotional atmosphere for action, and as the lag in comprehension grows, so do feelings of impotence and hostility. The public is also put off by what seems excessive zeal by the scientific community to guard its own interests. One hundred and fifty years ago Fourier criticized the use of specialized knowledge which separates people from the responsibility of social decisions. In many respects we face a standoff of academic versus populism, and it is this cleavage which must be resolved.

Partly, this develops because the public does not have ready access to the technical knowledge on which to make informed judgments. Such information is obscured by technical complexity, shielded by military security, blocked by bureaucratic obstructionism, proprietary claims of industry and executive privilege. Such filters may operate at random. But a more direct source of disenfranchisement is the frequent alliance which joins bureaucrats at the engines of government in a narrow symbiotic relationship with technocrats in industry and with their congressional patrons.

Except for those professionally engaged, very few citizens really understand science, and the reciprocal comprehension by natural scientists of the deeper needs, wants and dynamic processes of society is at best spotty. Since World War II and the advent of technological wonders for military application, and especially since the space race ignited in 1957, the news media have devoted more space to public understanding of science. Most contributions, however, have been of the "gee whiz" genre, intended to amuse and titillate but not to inform. Only recently in the aftermath of environmental concerns have there been thoughtful essays treating social consequences of technology. With subject matter all too often chosen in terms of the sensational, a benighted public desperately turns to government, demanding the use of its clumsy power of regulation.

This is not to say that the citizen is indifferent to the technical artifacts emanating from science. On the contrary, citizens continuously experience technology. In just the first few hours each day, individuals may be awakened by a radio alarm clock; climb out from an electric blanket; start coffee automatically percolating; begin breakfast with cereal from a box describing contents that resemble a chemical formula; drive on congested freeways to the office alone in a high-powered gas guzzler, with cues from helicopter-spotting traffic reports; park on the seventh floor of a garage, go the rest of the way to the office by elevator, then past clerks with desk top mini-computers in time to receive a long distance, satellite-relayed, phone call from seven time zones away. This equipment for living is taken for granted. Indeed, each year, new technologically-based adult toys make their appearance, aggressively merchandized by the manufacturers, but no less eagerly sought by a population that has come to depend on and expect the wonders of science to spin new miracles to gratify sensory (and, some psychologists would contend, adolescent) appetites.

With that deep penetration of technology into every waking (and with sleeping pills, even sleeping) moment of Westerners, we are compelled to ask how many of the 168 hours each week does the average citizen devote to thinking about social effects of technological change, and to asserting some element of personal responsibility for at least raising questions of future impact?

Meeting needs for public understanding of science was adopted as federal policy in 1950 legislation creating the National Science Foundation. Whatever the initial motivation, that function was given low priority, tending to be interpreted as the opportunity to recruit popular acceptance of more funding for research. On the basis of currently low levels of citizen comprehension, that original NSF program can hardly be viewed as successful. Several new programs open prospects but have not yet dented the problem.

Where lies the blame? It is foolish to look for devils in this situation, to point the finger, for example, at the National Science Foundation. For how should we expect any federal program to buck a powerful cultural tide?

Huizinga unpeeled this issue almost half a century ago.[133] As he wrote, universal education and modern publicity, instead of raising the level of culture, have produced symptoms of devitalization and degeneration. Science as new knowledge has not settled into the culture, and the aggregate of discoveries cannot be equated to culture.

Among knowledge consumers, with everyone getting a taste of everything, there is depreciation of critical judgment. And that weakening of judgment has been accelerated by techniques of mass entertainment wherein participation slides from active to passive mode, speeding abdication of informed judgment to others. Everyone becomes a trivial, Monday morning quarterback.

There is neither the capacity to deal with future consequences of unwitting applications of science, nor is there the will.

As to the scientific community, it has considered its primary role as one of acquiring and extending knowledge, recognizing but leaving to others the roles both of educating the public as to social implications of science, and of exercising responsibility as to ways and means for adopting and controlling natural forces. The scientific community may also share in the blame for a weakening of an intellectual conscience that underpins critical discernment.[134]

Granted, various groups of scientists have become crusaders for arms control and for environmental conservancy. A few have tackled broader questions of survival. While not identified with causes as such, other scientists have become activists in their own community, applying their expertise to local issues of nuclear power, toxic substances, etc., and to regulation of research on design and production of artificial genes.

Professional organizations also now get involved. Journals have carried articles on key policy issues to enlighten members. Some organizations have confirmed validity of their tax exempt status, then buttoned up their courage by taking public positions, submitting testimony and stepping up attention to professional activities in which ethical dimensions of social responsibilities are at stake. The concepts of technology assessment have begun to be integrated into professional engineering practice and teaching. At the October 1977 meeting of the American Society of Civil Engineers, nearly 20 per cent of the 300 technical papers dealt with aspects of impact analysis compared to perhaps 2 per cent in 1962. By such initiatives, engineers are accepting the fact that in a profession licensed by law to practice, they bear a social responsibility that parallels the lawyer's role as a friend of the court and the physician as public health officer. In their practice, engineers are, analogously, counselors to the public. They could facilitate citizen awareness and enlightenment on alternatives in technology-intensive public policy and the consequences of each.[135]

Looking ahead, the scientific and engineering communities could be of more direct assistance through heavier commitment of their professional societies to public interest activities and to citizen understanding. At present, organizations of both scientists and engineers devote the greatest fraction of their income from dues to dissemination of technical information to each other through journals and conferences. The public is never excluded, but the content and style of such communication is so highly specialized as to discourage participation by any but the expert.

The scientific community and engineering professions have an unfulfilled obligation to reconsider their function in a technological society, to devote a larger fraction of effort collectively and individually to helping the other 98 per cent of the population who are nonspecialists to grasp the technical foundations to modern life and associated threats to survival.[136]

Some of this difficulty arises from cultural isolation of the scientific and engineering communities. One antidote lies in a more systematic exposure to issues that concern society generally, especially regarding those whose lives seldom intersect with the technical aristocracy, and whose consequently remote concerns and dreams are alien and heard vicariously, if at all. When the technical community asserts greater interest in technology assessment and recognizes that it must address the stark questions of who wins, who loses, and how much, then they may also recognize that the attack on these questions of cultural and psychological as well as operational effects involves a kaleidoscopic blend of technical with social knowledge. The first ingredient that is taken for granted, and the reinforcement of the second, will not likely turn a mechanical engineer into a seasoned social philosopher. But it surely will widen the perspective and enrich the value base which is intrinsically present in all judgments that the technical community is called upon to make on technology-intensive public policy.

This integration of technical with social considerations reflects a reality that purely technical ingredients cannot be readily separated out for evaluation. In technically based issues, the political and social value elements are almost always more powerful in relation to socially satisfactory outcomes than the technical. Indeed, the very process of separation involves value choices, so that the notion of separation may not be feasible and may even be undesirable.

Nevertheless, this notion of separation is at the heart of a concept for a "science court" widely discussed in the scientific community in 1976. As proposed by Arthur Kantrowitz,[137] the court would be created as a new institution to debate technical questions associated with controversial public policy issues on which scientists disagree. By use of an adversary proceeding presided over by an impartial panel of scientific judges to resolve conflicts over facts, judgments would be issued with "sufficient presumptive validity to provide an improved base on which political decisions could be reached through the democratic process."

Critics of this proposal point out that such a body could not escape being considered a political institution, no matter how much isolation proponents may wish, and that it might facilitate a cop-out of decision makers by misdirecting attention from the issues. Also, establishment of a court by edict might weaken the health of the scientific enterprise and run counter to the science ethos, then create illusions of certainty where none exists. As it relates to the questions raised here, a science court could accelerate a government by experts, widen the cleavage between scientists and citizens, and not address needs of deeper public understanding of science. On the main objective of fact–value separation, Barry M. Casper wrote that "our present institutions for involving scientists in public policy decision making already tend to bring about this separation of and overemphasis on technical matters. This tendency is a major contributor to the current syndrome of crisis reaction, narrow technical debate, and presumed 'technical fixes' which fail to address basic long range problems."[138]

The crux of the matter is that scientists and engineers must ease the temptation to believe that only people with sophisticated technical backgrounds can deal with technology policy. They must come to recognize that the greater the expertise, experience and involvement with the purely technical details the more an individual scientist and engineer is likely to lose objectivity, inadvertently to become aligned with political forces and institutions in which he or she is associated because of having a stake in the outcome. Indeed, what the expert most needs is a faith in the democratic process where the fundamental choices are public choices among clearly presented options, and where the scientific community's first—not last—obligation is to fortify public understanding.

It is in this interaction that scientists and engineers may begin to appreciate what other intellectual, social, ethical and human considerations enter the policy process, to learn that life, unlike science, has perpetual ambiguity, and to find joys of stimulation as well as enlightenment from the wisdom if not knowledge of nonscientists. In bringing together those concerned largely with means and those concerned largely with ends, interest could well be rekindled in the scientific community of dedication to a higher abstract principle.

Mutual diffusion of knowledge and points of view would help counter the cultural tilt toward the short term. Fruits of direct scientist–citizen interaction may be realized by enhanced quality of citizen participation more than by quantity.

One result could be a political constituency for the future.

Prizes of Anticipation: Crisis Avoidance by Technology Assessment

Consideration of the future has frequently been translated as long range planning, but simply more long range planning is unpromising. While sector by sector functional planning is both desirable and feasible, master blueprinting as has been advocated for so long has backfired in unexpected outcomes. For one thing, there is no agreement on paradise. For another, planning has usually been conceived as isolated from doing, removed from dimensions of reality, immune to kinetics of change and unmindful of systematic feedback for course correction. Many forecasting models do not work. Others only goad technology to self-fulfilling prophecy. And people want to plan for themselves; they like to make choices. The pursuit of happiness may offer joys not always found in its ultimate attainment. Rigid planning that eliminates the unexpected may prove psychologically dull.

There is another way, however, of looking ahead. The notion of posting sentries to reduce surprise is certainly as old as warfare. As it relates to survival, this constitutes deliberate and organized vigilance.

Put another way, the emphasis is on prevention—catastrophe prevention. And the technique of metaphorical preventative medicine is crisis avoidance by technology assessment (TA).

Basic precepts have been advocated by a number of social critics. Brzezinski said in 1967 that "our existing post-crisis management institutions will probably be increasingly supplanted by pre-crisis management institutions, the task of which will be to identify in advance likely social crises and to develop programs to cope with them."[139] Stuart Chase visualized a supranational Bureau of Standards "to evaluate and screen consequences of large technological innovations before they go into mass production, seriously to affect the culture."[140] Toffler called for a technology ombudsman in an anticipatory democracy.[141] Meadows *et al.* call for long term assessment to mitigate ultimately crushing limits to growth.[142] Califano has proposed a presidential-powers impact statement to elucidate consequences of new legislation.[143]

Because this notion of anticipatory assessment has found its way into major new U.S. legislation, that process deserves examination as an important political experiment. Beginning about 1965, an unusual initiative began in the U.S. Congress to encourage systematic anticipatory analysis in legislative affairs. Under leadership of Emilio Q. Daddario, then Chairman of the House of Representatives Subcommittee on Science, Research and Development, with assistance from the Congressional Research Service,[144] a series of bills was introduced, hearings were conducted and consultative studies inaugurated by the National Academies of Science, of Engineering and of Public Administration. They culminated with signing into law on October 13, 1972, the Technology Assessment Act of 1972, PL 92–484.

As to its purpose, this measure asserted in Section 2(b) ". . . that, to the fullest extent possible, the consequences of technological applications be anticipated, understood, and considered in determination of public policy on existing and emerging national problems." Thus was enacted the first piece of legislation directed to systematic technology-related vigilance.

As to the basic concept of technology assessment, it was considered as an early warning system, based on the question, What if? It was to operate as an aid to decision making by inventorying all technical and social alternative strategies that could be conceived to meet a particular policy objective, drawing on a blend of technical fact and social values. And it was to furnish a rational basis for choice by laying out all plausible consequences of each. Technology assessment could thus dissolve the widely recognized myopia in the decision theater by looking sideways at impacts beyond the usual boundaries of the technological transaction and by looking ahead at future developments and ways to preserve future choice.

A wide range of well-exercised methodologies was available to those preparing assessments, derived from economic cost–benefit analysis, engineering systems analysis, polling and other social science research techniques.[(145)] Most scholars in the field agreed that a base of fact was necessary but not sufficient. A fertile imagination was essential to generate the vectors of action and their impacts, a holistic, multidisciplinary problem rather than discipline-oriented inquiry. Thus involved were heuristic, qualitative rather than quantitative techniques.

By and large, TA would supplement decision judgment by making explicit a range of implicit factors that were neglected, undervalued or treated at random. It could identify what we do know; what we do not know; what we could know; and what we should know. In that sense, TA could identify additional scientific and engineering research (indeed, new technical options) that could expand the range of alternatives or reduce uncertainty. This source of nominations introduces a novel twist on research proposals by scientists on the basis of gaps in the state of knowledge at disciplinary frontiers, or by engineers requiring information to make their machines work.

From the outset, technology assessment was viewed as an element in legal and political process in its potential to illuminate who wins and who loses and how much. And more than an elegant planning device, its value was felt to be in reducing the range and vagueness of risk, to limit penalties of narrow choice and improve the allocation of public resources.

Among the more optimistic advocates, TA could compensate for inadequacies of political process through which implications for the unrepresented are often ignored because political bargaining minimizes costs only to the obvious parties at interest.

By timely and open publication of assessments, issues and options could be examined by all holding a stake in the outcome, shortening the lag in public information and perceptions, and possibly altering the response. As shown in Fig. 1, technology assessment was thought to be a new avenue of social feedback with potential to serve not just government but all participants in the system.[146]

Nevertheless, a deliberate modesty is necessary with regard to TA expectations. It would not tell decision makers what to do, only what to explore.

Given the expectations and prospects accorded this unprecedented technology assessment legislation, its implementation and subsequent influence warrant elaboration. The Act created a triad of implementing bodies: an oversight Technology Assessment Board of six senators and six representatives, an operations Office of Technology Assessment, and a Technology Assessment Advisory Council composed of ten, part-time outsiders plus the heads of the two existing major staff agencies to Congress, the Government Accounting Office (GAO) and the Congressional Research Service (CRS). Functions of OTA itself were spelled out, comprising then, and still, a compact and useful definition of technology assessment itself.

In the exact wording of Section 3(c), OTA was called upon to:

(1) identify existing or probable impacts of technology or technological programs;
(2) where possible, ascertain cause-and-effect relationships;
(3) identify alternative technological methods of implementing specific programs;
(4) identify alternative programs for achieving requisite goals;
(5) make estimates and comparisons of the impacts of alternative methods and programs;
(6) present findings of completed analyses to the appropriate legislative authorities;
(7) identify areas where additional research or data collection is

required to provide adequate support for the assessments, and estimates described in paragraph (1) through (5) of this subsection; and

(8) undertake such additional associated activities as the appropriate authorities specified under subsection (d) may direct.

By way of historical perspective, one of the initial motivations of the bill's sponsors was to apply this mode of policy research to ferret out and promote underutilized technology and human resources freed by a tapering off of the United States space program. Soon after, that thrust was sharply altered by a public consciousness and a public conscience over possibly adverse environmental impacts of such initiatives. Concerns over side effects swiftly captured political attention. However, this concept of environmental assessment raised jurisdictional questions with other House committees. This sector of TA was then siphoned off in 1969, following precepts of congressional advisor Lynton Caldwell. It became a prominent and provocative Section 102(2)c of the National Environmental Policy Act requiring environmental impact statements. Many individual states have followed with environmental assessment processes of their own.

Meanwhile, social and economic repercussions of technology, as well as environmental, began to capture public attention and concern, spearheaded by Ralph Nader and by the activist New Left. Technology was blindly attacked as villain by some, but more widely as being employed without social responsibility. As a result, initial purposes of the technology assessment legislation were somewhat changed to its final thrust. Even then, the legislation failed to stimulate much congressional interest, found few champions and aroused legislators' passions largely over jurisdictional conflicts within the House, over routine House–Senate wrangling, and over questions of separation of powers with the President as to appointment procedures of public Council members. After legislation was passed but before funds were approved, Senator Edward Kennedy declared a long standing interest in the function, and as the ranking Democratic senator appointed to TAB, became the activity's chief congressional steward from 1973 to 1974, and again in 1977–1978.

Creation of OTA had a number of immediate effects outside of

Congress. The small band of determined advocates in academia and public interest movements found a highly visible symbol of tough-minded futures studies to rally around. The National Science Foundation was better able to justify its modest and internally unpopular grant program in technology assessment. Private consulting organizations engaged in futures research found it helpful to ride the crest of this new wave. Professional societies, especially in engineering, began to consider the relevance of social responsibilities in practice, and a number of engineering colleges began to offer formal courses in TA. Limited echoes were heard from abroad, especially from Japan, where environmental malfeasance suddenly became a topic for hot debate.

When OTA was formally switched on in 1973, Emilio Daddario, then a retired congressman, was appointed by TAB as director. OTA sought and received liberal budgets, and aggressively advertised itself not only as a congressional staff arm but as the intellectual focus of a TA movement. It sponsored a series of large contract studies and added staff. By November 1978 annual budgets were on the order of $11 million; staff numbered 140. Reports began to emerge and be utilized by Congress, covering such topics as bioequivalence of drugs, prospects of solar energy and an evaluation of ERDA's research portfolio, impacts along the Delaware–New Jersey coast of offshore oil drilling and of floating nuclear power plants, oil tanker safety and needs for better information systems to enhance food production.

But there was also released an unprecedented series of public critiques of OTA. They were prepared by an outgoing chairman of the Advisory Council, Harold Brown, then President of California Institute of Technology, by a former staffer turned policy analyst, and by three congressional committees or study bodies with oversight responsibilities.[147] All underscored the youth and novelty of the operation and recognized start-up difficulties. In generally guarded language, however, performance was criticized. Management was said to be weak; duplication in functions appeared with sister agencies GAO and CRS; independence and objectivity of studies were uncertain. Staff were said to be overpaid and underqualified. Without tenure, none were protected from intimidation for being candid on hot issues; some depended for their appointment upon political allegiances to individual members of Congress. Assessments in disproportionate number originated from TAB members, focused on currently debated rather than long term issues, and framed as general policy studies rather than technology assessments performed with the rigorous methodology prescribed by statute. Few published assessments laid out alternatives, differentiated impacts and impacted parties, traced consequences, analyzed cause and effect or pinpointed research to lower uncertainty. Most of all, the OTA started off by yielding to intense pressures for attention to the short run.

Although not discussed by these critiques, the Technology Assessment Board did not become an early warning arm of the Congress. It dealt largely with internal OTA management. Interest by board members was mixed and declined further during 1975–1976 when the TAB Chairman, Olin Teague, fell ill. Recommendations for correctives offered by the Advisory Council were stubbornly turned aside by the OTA director. Indeed, the Council which is the first continuing advisory unit ever created by Congress for its own use was remarkably ineffective.

One fundamental question did emerge. The organic legislation was sufficiently broad that two different modes of implementation were possible. One was to cast the operation in the style of a new joint committee of the Congress, with OTA functioning somewhat as committee staff. A second possibility was to emulate the style of GAO and CRS, serving all members of Congress equitably, avoiding political ties, and building staffs on the basis of competence and integrity and devoid of loyalties to individual members.

It was Mr. Daddario's judgment to opt for the first, in the belief that only by such identity would the Office elicit support from the initially small cadre of OTA backers. Criticism of OTA brings into question the wisdom of that choice. After he resigned in July 1977, and a new director recruited, the question of style was reopened. Indeed, a new opportunity was presented to Congress to review the entire OTA experience and consider major reforms.(148) Russell Peterson, previously Governor of Delaware and Chairman of the Council on Environmental Quality, was appointed as director in January 1978.

The authority to hire and fire staff was delegated by TAB entirely to the OTA director. The internal structure was reorganized so that substantive responsibility was more effectively shared by senior staff.

Some unfruitful lines of policy research were terminated, and an entirely new thrust mounted to change the mix of assessments with a better balance of long with short range issues and, as mentioned before, an outside dragnet was conducted for nominations of key topics. Clearly, a shift in style has emerged that portends an upgrading in quality and in the early warning function visualized by original backers.

The Congressional Technology Assessment Board might also consider reforming its role to serve its entire parent body as an early warning system, perhaps as the Joint Congressional Committee for the Future proposed by Michael Harrington.[149] Such a committee would differ from its brethren in not serving a specialized function or narrow constituency. TAB could compensate for the political practices of crisis management that overwhelm other committees, by dealing with most salient and overarching questions of survival. It could assist leadership in both Houses to determine which issues on the current agenda have the most serious portents and thus help sort out priorities. Then Congress could invest time in some proportion to severity of consequences, rather than in proportion to pressure and rhetoric.[150] Attention could be focused on the important and not merely urgent.

Under any circumstances, making OTA work is exceedingly difficult. Most leaders in the assessment movement had cautioned about the primitive nature of this decision aid, the need for modesty in conclusions and the inevitability of uncertainty. There was also concern that too much emphasis was placed on the technique ingredient of technology, unbalanced by consideration of how past institutional decisions, commitments and behavior influence the social functioning of a technological system. That is, assessments tended to overlook the strengths, weaknesses and options as to systems which determine and execute the programs, the internal and external milieu, the motivations of different actors and potential shifts in the cultural setting.

Finally, there were warnings that investigating consequences is inherently political, vulnerable to political biases and constraints. The SST cut-off, discussed previously, is such an example.

Concerns have also been aired over weaknesses of social and governmental organizations in utilizing assessments when completed because of the resistance of organic institutional structures to change. Both before and after Congress established OTA, cautions were offered on limitations to their genuine curiosity as to impacts, and of the tendency of members to undertake only "safe" studies because of challenges to their announced positions when OTA reports are made public. A major question was raised as to the political appetite for rationality, indeed, skepticism as to whether or not TA's will enter the decision theater as to be influential in sharpening the process of choice.

To answer these doubts, a recent study under sponsorship of the National Science Foundation has been completed at the University of Michigan of 28 TA's produced under NSF support and 5 by OTA; 280 users who claim to be familiar with one or more of these were interviewed by telephone, and 48 involved in the production of TA's were interviewed face to face. The purpose was to discover how the characteristics of TA, including the process of interaction with potential users and means for dissemination, affect their utilization for policy making in a variety of settings. From such insights it was hoped to develop procedures that would improve their utility in the future.

The study found that by and large the TA's in the sample were *not* being widely used or proving influential. Other results indicated that:

(1) Lack of use was due to inappropriate timing. The TA arrived either too late to influence perceptions and actions already committed, or too early to elicit attention above the noise level of other crises.

(2) The level of utilization was highest in the legislative branch of government, which tends to be the least knowledgeable about the issues, and least used by those whose self-estimates of knowledgeability was high. Interestingly enough, potential users in business and industry felt especially knowledgeable about the issues prior to receiving the TA's and were the least interested in the findings.

(3) Findings of the TA were ignored when felt to be incompatible with institutional self-interest. Both the producers of TA's and potential users agreed that the products have strong political implications for user organizations. That is, TA's could have favorable or unfavorable impacts on the interests or the preferred approaches of their organizations, and this matter is dealt with in greater detail subsequently.

(4) The greater the uncertainty and speculation in a TA, the less the utilization.

(5) The longer persons have been in an organization, the less likely they are to use it.

(6) The higher the credibility of the methodology employed, the greater the probability of utilization.

(7) The greater the completeness in statement of facts and underlying assumptions, the greater the utility.

(8) The style, format and length affected the usefulness.

It was also found that more use was made of TA's having a short time perspective and explicitly focused on political issues that were already boiling, a matter that is paradoxically in conflict with the basic notion of a TA to extend time horizons and provide unbiased early warning about the consequences of long term impacts.

The potential role of early warning in public decision process has steadily increased since 1965. Apart from creating OTA, the Congress has established yet another staff arm—the Congressional Budget Office—both to impart overall coherence to the budget as a national priority list and to force attention to future obligations associated with current decisions. The Congress in 1972 mandated its committees to include a future orientation and requested the Congressional Research Service to reinforce its capabilities for futures studies. And the GAO on its own initiative has more self-consciously examined policy implications of current trends. But the total effect of these intentions in dealing with survival-threatening issues is piecemeal, episodic and unmatched to the situation.

Meanwhile, as far as the art of anticipation itself is concerned, much has been published. Apart from a few excellent compendia, contributions are seldom distinguished by heft or originality. The intellectual core that was the province of academic scholarship has not been conspicuously strengthened. Indeed, NSF funding to build a necessary foundation of scholarship has been unsteady, pegged at a parsimonious $1.3 million annually.

Few examples are available of completed assessments that meet the criteria for impact analysis. Most seriously, none that dealt with public policy weighed political consequences of the type outlined earlier. OTA steered decorously clear of such sensitive ingredients. So do analyses funded by executive branch agencies, usually under instruction by the sponsor.

The result is to leave the potential of TA unfulfilled and to deprive the Congress of ways to counter being outgunned by the executive branch's experts with, as Etzioni notes, its virtual monopoly over state-generated information and analysis.[151] It is also clear that if the Congress is to fulfill its constitutional responsibilities, some major changes in congressional decision attitudes are needed to circumvent classical political games.

From this account, it is clear that neither the executive nor the legislative branches have a sound and well exercised capability for crisis modification by technology assessment. Even in those cases of completed studies, utilization seems feeble. The reader might justifiably question, in view of the flutter and flounce of OTA and a non-start in OSTP, why the author remains a stubborn advocate.

The mere fact that OTA survived such unprecedented public criticism and still gains congressional support is strong evidence that others share this view: the promise of TA has never been adequately tested as to its potency as an aid to decision making. Yet its role grows more urgent. Under whatever label, it is increasingly difficult to steer technology where both its artifacts and its policies so forcefully condition the future. For all the reasons advanced throughout this essay we dare not do without a systematic exploration of longer term consequences and their assessment in the calculus of present choice. In that step, again we recall that we refer to collective choice. Technology assessments, promptly shared, become key instruments to widen public appreciation of the issues.

Interinstitutional Networks: A Metaphoric Fourth Branch of Government

New social learning to enhance vision and counter political limits in steering technology boils down to five imperatives:

—expanding and deepening social awareness of the future, of consequences of present myopia, and of predicaments that, untended, challenge survival;

—enriching the cultural framework in a technological society by a shift in values: rethinking commitment to uncritical economic growth as the midwife of progress; resisting the turn-on of instant

sensory satisfactions; encouraging political and commercial institutions to balance short run with long run interests;
—strengthening foresight and analysis to anticipate pernicious effects or unmet opportunities of technology and to facilitate collision avoidance;
—reinforcing citizen intervention in the political process so as to enhance responsiveness and accountability of government, aided by coalitions with the scientific–engineering community;
—making better use of communications techniques for exchange of information, both technical and social, among all parties involved or impacted by technological enterprise.

None of these canons of procedure can be invoked without resources, human, financial and institutional. And whatever the reforms generated in separate institutions, their social effectiveness lies in recognizing a mutually reinforcing synergism as a network: linkages among citizens, public interest groups, universities, libraries, museums, nonprofit research institutes, the scientific and engineering community, industry and government.

Critically needed is a credible, vigorous and accessible instrument for technology assessment, including the mechanics of public dissemination. Despite legislation to equip the U.S. Congress and the President with TA advisory units, as has been said, neither OTA nor OSTP is yet moving energetically or with commitment to fulfill its promise. A more damaging shortfall, however, is that the public has little or no access to the anticipatory information regarding impacts. For a congressional staff arm to release candid findings on highly sensitive issues is to invite budgetary retaliation from offended members in congressional hot seats. The President's staff are similarly constricted; products of their research which detail the politics of an issue as well as substance may be impounded legitimately by executive privilege.

Following earlier arguments, an early warning device must be independent of political constraints: in staff selection, in choice of topics evaluated, in range of alternatives and of consequences including political, in objectivity, in freedom to come to unpopular, even radical, conclusions and in unself-serving dissemination.

There is a long history of proposals to equip the U.S. Government with such an analytical capability. Rexford Tugwell was one such author in the 1930s. In fact, a National Resources Planning Board was once established with similar, albeit specialized, functions, but in the bureaucratic infighting over implications of the facts, it was snuffed out. A broader concept was subsequently advanced by Nicholas Golovin,[152] cast in terms of a new "evaluative" function. Then, in 1970, a specific proposal was laid before the House Subcommittee on Science, Research and Development for a technology assessment capability independent of Congress and the White House. It was termed a fourth branch of government by the subcommittee chairman.[153] This notion was translated to draft legislation, S. 4044, introduced by Senator Warren G. Magnuson, cast in terms of a Commission for the Social Management of Technology. Subsequently, the concept was challenged on grounds that independence of such a unit would be bought at the price of political isolation; without power, it would be impotent. Questions were also raised about nomination procedures to the Commission (by the Supreme Court from a list of candidates advanced by citizens and professional groups to blend technical competencies and social perspectives); its source of power (primarily the power of information but also the right to sue government agencies for failure to carry out mandated functions); its source of funds (an endowment of 10 years by the Congress); its dissemination of reports (to the public, industry and government).

The key point is that careful impact assessments available to all parties at interest would provide social feedback, operating through many legitimate political channels. But that proposition got nowhere. Some years later, Alton Frye and colleagues proposed an Institute for the Congress with similar functions. As a guarantee of independence, it would be funded from private foundation sources. In 1978 advocates were still hopeful of its creation.

Meanwhile, independent assessment is carried out piecemeal by a covey of public interest groups. The difficulty is that many rock along on meager funds, tackle issues of high visibility and thus of more immediate political concern that inflame passions and stretch objectivity of researchers, deal with symptoms rather than root causes, lack funds for stable expert staffs, often fail to communicate with each other, depend on a constituency of the disaffected, have limited energies to tackle the broader but less certain perils, often lose credibility because they are obliged to be self-serving, and end up inadvertently labeled as ideological technology arrestors and thus not respected as independent evaluators.

Nevertheless, the collective impact of these groups is impressive. The environmental movement has nudged the nation and its political leaders to assure a stewardship for the natural world. And like all significant movements in history they provide the psychological energy for value shifts. Far from replacing these groups, any new technology assessment operation would simply provide information for activists to employ in legitimate and decorous lobbying.[154]

But a fourth branch, if that metaphor is to be employed, is not best distinguished as another block on an organization chart. It would not require a constitutional amendment. Rather, to facilitate existing constitutional purposes, it would comprise an interinstitutional network. Its function would be to integrate independent analytical capabilities with existing units and develop linkages between geographically dispersed and varied sources and clients.[155]

Although such an aid to social choice would make use of the TA concept, a "fourth branch" should be thought of more as an "appreciative" function than as evaluative. Its first task would be to facilitate social learning to deal with the most fundamental challenges of survival.

On the question of funds, Ralph Nader and, separately, a committee of the National Commission on Supplies and Strategies in December 1976 recommended the use of tax deductions as modest contributions to organizations seeking to influence governmental decisions. In different form, a new NSF grant program was proposed by Senator Edward Kennedy.[156]

Using either funding source, a different proposition is advanced here, to utilize such funds only for a citizens' information network that is universally accessible, but which in itself is not permitted to be an advocate.

Comparable channels of information are already in place for worldwide instantaneous communications regarding military affairs, the weather, and banking. Scientists talk to scientists worldwide through data banks, journals, mail and cloakroom chitchat at professional meetings. The technology of networking is available and could supplement the information now reaching citizens through the media. It would have clear assets in its collective memory. In its access to outlying provinces, it could provide timely schedules on pending national legislation, so avidly collected by vested interests and Washington lobbyists. People would not only know what is going on, but where to intervene and when. The hope would be that they would then demand anticipatory rather than reactive politics.

In a sense, too, citizens could help each other so that studies of local issues could be employed by other parties contending with the same issue in different regions.

Without such networks of shared information to counter various elements of our society losing track of each other, the advantages of pluralism may be dissolved. Says John Gardner,[157] a society that is capable of conscious self-renewal must have effective internal communication among its diverse elements.

In short, the issue is how to provide a blend of technical information, of signals of the future and of value preferences to the governed to help them participate in governance. Citizens could then play an energetic and legitimate political role to determine what long range questions should be balanced with the short range, and to do it "in time to allow them to influence policy-oriented deliberation."[158]

Mechanisms for Conflict Resolution

It is generally agreed that because social preferences in the body politic vary, government has the primary role of integration. But it has also been emphasized that self-interests of public and private institutions stimulate conflict. As these become politically potent, a highly charged, adversarial culture seems to be in the making. For one thing, the courts are seriously overloaded. There is a proclivity to joust rather than arbitrate. Projects having environmental overtones have been delayed or stopped but, ironically, largely on procedural grounds. That is, the primary legal basis for objections to technological initiatives has not been the severity of adverse impact anticipated, but simply shortcomings in the preparation of the Section 102(2)c impact statement.

Some of these delays have been therapeutic. With the Trans-Alaska Pipeline, for example, engineering to meet damage to permafrost from pipe carrying hot oil was vastly improved during the years of litigation. But the scars of combat during this process left the Alyeska Pipeline Company and the environmentalists bitter and exhausted.

Clearly, the courts have a role. But reliance on this mechanism of conflict resolution is exacting higher and higher transaction costs.

We are thus confronted with yet another powerful dilemma. On the one hand, there are growing threats to public health and safety that contemporary social mores will not accept. On the other hand, we find that processes of regulation to protect the public may inadvertently impede overall social performance. Regulations frequently lag technological change so that we breathlessly play catch-up. Correctives then soak up capital that otherwise might be invested in creative innovation, pointing up, incidentally, the hidden costs of opportunistic incrementalism. Regulations become cumulative, introducing more constraints that reduce tolerance for diversity, for example, in different regions not being permitted options for meeting locally differentiated risks of pollution. These constraints add to the already high levels of social complexity and to the stress of conflicting values that were found earlier to distort the balance of long versus short run outlooks.

When these conflicts fail to be resolved early, they fester to be played out as strenuous contests on the political stage at the end of deliberation. By that time, positions of adversaries are hard, hot and stubbornly defended because so much ego is then at stake.

Ironically, in a government so admired as one of law rather than of men, it is mechanical legalism and the adversarial process in practice that often booby-trap social performance of technology. The emotionally charged atmosphere, assessment of blame, search for villains and enhancement of a "siege" mentality dominate decision making. Contestants forget that the key issue is social acceptance of risk, rather than its elimination or neglect.

Clearly, there is a crying need to develop more congenial procedures. The question, then, is how to create a pre-crisis problem-solving atmosphere. Such an evolution requires first of all a mutual survey of the situation, the facts and the alternatives. Affected parties with different perspectives and interests would have opportunities to intervene. Past practice in the spirit of arbitration and compromise has headed off bruising contests between labor and management, and even some nasty international conflicts. It deserves renewed dedication.

To generate a problem-solving mood, however, requires preparation. Industry in particular needs to recognize the changes in values that underlie policy constraints to its historical freedoms. One route to harmony lies in anticipatory analysis by each contender to identify conflicts before they reach typical stages of ignition, steam rollering of dissent and shouting. For with a high noise level, everyone loses a hearing capability for signals about the future in which all parties share a common destiny.

CHAPTER 9

Margins for Survival

Engineering Lessons for Public Safety

Five new strategies for technological choice just outlined constitute a design for survival. This design is not focused on individual threats, no matter how ominous, but rather on another pervasive and perhaps most trenchant danger—weakening of the social decision apparatus to the point that we are unable to choose.

That way of thinking about the problem itself provokes curiosity in lessons to be extracted from analogous endeavors. Called to mind are elements of engineering practice that include design for public safety. The simile may be particularly apt in resolving parallel enigmas of human error, human ignorance and lack of imagination.

Virtually all technological artifacts are engineered. By that we mean that buildings, dams, engines, automobiles, telephones, kitchen aids and even some toys are systematically planned to meet a prescribed function; they are then designed, proportioned and constructed in accordance with engineering principles derived from natural sciences and with rules derived from empirical experience. Among these rules of practice is the application of a margin for safety.

In social terms, the safety margin is an act of professional responsibility to protect the user and the public from bodily harm, functional inconvenience or economic loss. In technical terms, the safety margin is introduced as an arbitrary multiple of the expected or specified loading to reduce perceived risk to socially acceptable levels. If a floor in a building is expected to carry heavy files weighing, say, 40 pounds per square foot, the joists, beams, girders, columns and footings may be proportioned larger as though the loading were 160. Or if an auto axle is expected during a lifetime to undergo bending in rotation so as to induce fatigue cracks in 10 million cycles, it is designed instead to sustain 100 million. As a result, the structure, machine or component will be made several times larger in physical size or in performance capacity than one designed to sustain only the expected load.

By this technique, the engineer accommodates uncertainties—uncertainties of environmental exposure, loads, properties of materials employed, of quality control in fabrication, maintenance and effects of aging. He or she compensates for fallibility of inadequate knowledge in the application of engineering principles or behavior of the system never previously built at that scale, offsetting any lack of imagination and unknowns as to statistical likelihood of environmental hazard such as earthquakes. Also taken into account are risks of human abuse of the product, idiocy, mischief and blunder.

It must be emphasized, however, that safety margins are selected by pragmatic judgment, strongly influenced by the exercise of social responsibility. During the effervescent age of invention in the 19th century, margins were developed empirically from dramatic experiences of failure, for example, in explosions of steam boilers.

If the consequences of failure are severe, greater precision may be used in design or care in execution. Or safety margins may be increased. Or the system designed with fail-safe redundancy to accommodate component malfunction without disastrous overall collapse. In the case of submarine design, for example, the thin metal shell of a hull must be strong enough to sustain the external hydrostatic pressure imposed during a deep dive. Otherwise, failure would almost certainly be catastrophic and lethal. Accordingly, a high factor of safety is indicated, perhaps as high as used in commercial pressure vessels. Yet, with such precautions, the hull would be so heavy as to penalize submarine performance in range, speed or weapon-carrying capacity. To meet this dilemma, an extraordinarily low factor of safety is employed, but compensated by zealous precision in design, with methods refined by extensive basic and applied research, and confirmed by tests of scale models. The hull is contructed with high quality control, watchmaker care as to structural circularity, with welding integrity checked by x-ray. Then on its maiden voyage, the craft is driven below the surface in carefully controlled stages while hull strains are measured, once more to confirm safety of operation at the maximum intended depth, and, incidentally, to check the design methods themselves. Subsequent routine operation is expected to be disciplined so as never to exceed the depth limit.

Similarly skillful engineering design where weight–risk trade offs were strenuous are epitomized by success of the four manned lunar landings.

Even with these precautions there have been failures. In 1939 the Tacoma Narrows suspension bridge in the State of Washington was set into self-excited vibration by high winds, leading to collapse. The cause was lack of imagination as to these wind effects because bridges had never previously displayed this aerodynamic instability. In 1977 a large oil spill in the North Sea resulted from human error in drilling procedure on the Bravo rig. In 1976 a major air collision resulted from human error in air traffic control. In 1975 the Teton Dam failed in Idaho due to an oversight of geological weaknesses at its juncture with the canyon.

There are no absolute guarantees against failure; only probabilities. Nevertheless, the high performance record of engineering products suggests the utility of safety-margin concepts in socioeconomic–political enterprise, explicitly to reduce risk of the futures people do not want.

One last point. A direct uncritical analogy of the engineering safety margin is not intended. For one thing, engineers enjoy a solitary opportunity in design to inject margins of safety. For the risks described here, society has many opportunities. So, the engineering concept is only a way of thinking.

Overcoming political limits to steering technology for collective security may require three different margins for survival in strategies of technological choice: organized vigilance, resolute liquidity and counterpoises to the coercion of time. All of these have been discussed before, but for reasons of emphasis, they are summarized again as we consider not only where we are and where we are headed, but also what we should do.

Organized Vigilance: A Doctrine of Anticipation

The role of military intelligence as early warning is universally regarded as crucial to national security, especially for survival against surprise. It has, however, no civilian counterpart. Yet no other concept but determined and systematic vigilance by anticipatory analysis has the power to animate democratic government so as to prevent unwanted futures from happening. While technology assessment has the potential to buttress political decision making, its track record exists primarily with respect to environmental impact analysis of highly localized projects. What is at stake is a fresh commitment of political will and resources to this neglected function. It is unfortunate that in its formative years the Congressional Office of Technology Assessment had been devoting only a small fraction of its energies to the overriding longer term issues. Instead of OTA influencing Congress to reinforce its foresight, Congress forced OTA into its own short term habits. Ironically, the House Subcommittee on Science, Research and Technology reported in November 1978 that, even among members requesting OTA studies on urgent issues, only 37 percent had read the final product. As to presidential interest, firm directives were still lacking for the undermanned OSTP staff to undertake TA's called for in basic legislation. Their October 1978 report, prepared by NSF, was so unresponsive to the legislative mandate as to elicit a growing current of criticism.

Clearly, if organized vigilance is to have teeth, additional steps are needed:

(1) Congress should demand that existing legislation be effectively implemented; (2) new legislation should be introduced calling for assessment of long range social, economic, environmental and political consequences of action or inaction on major hazards looming ahead; (3) funds should be provided NSF to expand its pump priming of intellectual resources essential to undergird a new field.

To confirm the past failure of civilian intelligence to anticipate threatening situations and inform the public of options and their consequences, we have only to ponder the economic havoc wrought by the OPEC price rise.

The question of early warning is not simply generation of more anticipatory studies for decision making at the top. That is necessary but not sufficient. For one thing, much of the information needed for such studies is currently lacking. As was observed about technology assessments, apart from fashioning alternatives and tracing consequences, there is an obligation to clarify what we do know, what we do not know, what we should know and could know if specific research were undertaken to fill critical gaps in knowledge for policy making. Thus, a commitment to organized vigilance would necessarily strengthen interdisciplinary research capabilities in social as well as natural sciences.

Finally, the point needs making that all citizens are clients of such anticipatory studies. For unless there is an informed consensus on need for this public investment in the future, and for action on the implications, expecting political disposition to trade off short for longer run considerations is a form of political science fiction.

What is at stake is a doctrinal approach—a doctrine of anticipation. Here may lie the most fundamental of science policies to steer technology toward socially satisfactory outcomes, in the face of uncertainty, change, complexity and interdependence.

Resolute Liquidity

Few domestic actions have been taken to change civilian priorities at a major scale except in the face of a direct military challenge. Conspicuous exceptions are initiatives of President Roosevelt to deal with the economic depression of the 1930s, President Truman's policy for foreign aid and President Kennedy's Office of Economic Opportunity. Fortunately in the past there has been adequate time to recruit resources for the United States to meet nonmilitary threats without severe punishment for error or lack of imagination. That luxury of reaction time has disappeared. But so, apparently, have the reserves.

It is a paradox today that affluent societies have no more liquidity of resources to consider, much less effect, new or changing technological priorities than those societies less well off or even desperate.

One explanation for this condition of poverty is the very nature of technological enterprise—mobilized around narrow explicit goals; motivated to their achievement with an insatiable appetite for implementation. Because vested interest groups and individual technological delivery systems exert intense political pressures in this scramble, no resources remain unspoken for to meet the future, or even to pay lagging external costs of recent initiatives.

It will thus require heroic measures of political will to set resources aside for the uncertain future. To be sure, President Carter's proposals for sunset budgeting are aimed at this condition by requiring frequent rejustification of programs. But execution of that review may prove as unrewarding as an earlier accounting initiative of PPBS budgeting.

To set aside, say, 2 percent of budgets in all agencies as a hedge against the unknown may seem rational but today, with pressures for tax relief, it is politically impracticable. A beginning might be made, however, if the President's Office of Science and Technology Policy were able to control such a fraction of federal research and development funds, to invest on its own initiative in research enterprises related to issues of global survival.

Sooner or later, the present social quagmire must be bypassed. The sociopolitical system must recognize the urgency of contingency funding to prepare for inevitable change.

Offsetting the Coercion of Time

One of the major sources of decision stress is the coercion of time, the frenetic parade of issues demanding attention and undermining essential cogitation, even speculation. Whatever the inner protest at this parody of thoughtful choice, politicians feel compelled to march to the drumbeat of external forces while compromising quality for quantity. The analogy of safe auto driving comes immediately to mind: the threat–response sensations while driving swiftly and encountering ar unexpected sequence of road signs cautioning a variety of hazards. Safety demands one of two responses: slowing down or devoting greater attention to skillful driving. The latter choice is familiar; so is the attendant fatigue, gradual depreciation of response alacrity and especially of judgment when confronted with new types of surprise.

The alternative is to slow down. That strategy seems anachronistic in a day of speed. Yet reducing decision velocity by taking more time is the only sure way of dealing with the clock. Taking more time, that is, on those decisions having the most salient consequences, and especially those having portent for malignant irreversible effects: taking time to examine, for example, the worldwide expenditures of $1 billion per day for arms, the role of and opportunities for peace research and an evaluation of its virtual absence on the political agenda; taking time to permit messages to reach all parties in a technological delivery system; taking time to sample feedback from initial stages of implementation of a major program before making a full commitment, and otherwise synchronizing feedback of information with events. Especially important is the need to open windows in time dimensions and to search out the approaching threats to survival that have not yet reached the political stage. In this respect, fewer decisions could well beget better decisions.

CHAPTER 10

Global Security

One striking feature of contemporary peril is that, for the first time in history, all citizens of the planet are exposed to the same predicaments. While this condition sets the stage for collective security measures, our sense of reality indicates not only the absence of collaborative ethos, but also that discord and competition in a political world intensify certain of the perils. Yet few if any of the threats to survival recognized earlier can be approached by unilateral initiatives of any single nation, even if that will were evoked.

Although it may be shattering to many cherished beliefs, the American future, or that of any nation, is in no way under its exclusive control; there are many hands conning the helm of destiny.

A second commonality is also manifest. Decision making and decision makers in every society—capitalist, socialist or developing—are subject to the same dilemmas, constraints, pressures, scarcities of time and pathologies of the short run. Indeed, in developing nations with serious economic disadvantages, the long run is almost always discounted. Politicians widely recognize and respect the decision stress and personal pressures they share, whatever their confrontations over ideology. No wonder when they meet they are spontaneously moved to publicly embrace.

The interactions and interdependencies cited earlier for domestic institutions have a planetary companion. Facilitated by modern transport and communication, if not by political achievements, we have one world. Natural resources, manufactured goods, information and people freely cross the globe. So do pollutants in ocean and atmosphere. And so do ideas, the fads of the youth culture and the ethos of equality. It is an unmistakable record of history that a vigorous, post World War II technology energized this condition, worldwide.

That spurt also has side effects. With time and distance no longer insulating nation states and affording room for maneuver, opportunities for tension increase. And as images of affluence are spread in consumer products, and the mass media describe political freedom, those less well off instantly perceive their deprivation. Then they are stimulated positively to imitate or adapt, or negatively to nurse resentment.

Global political processes inevitably reflect this situation, with generally less rather than more stability. In just a few decades, the nation-state framework that evolved over centuries to structure international politics has been seriously eroded. As Brzezinski sees it,[(159)] spheres of influence, military alliances, the fiction of sovereignty and doctrinal conflicts arising from prior collisions are no longer valid. The era of perceived certainty reflected by the clash of ideology is gone. Even orthodox concepts of national interest are being squeezed, no longer based on geography, historic alliances or contests, economic self-interest, or on national security bought by arms.

By no means does this imply that nationalism is dead. Nowhere is its durability more convincingly revealed than on the stage of the United Nations. Rhetoric that can be readily forgiven in the adolescent stages of national identity is, however, translated into action.

It is starkly evident in the draft treaty generated by the U.N.'s third Law of the Sea Conference. Parenthetically, these deliberations over a period of six years were sparked initially by a lofty awareness that the oceans are essential to life on this planet and that both the use and abuse of the seas are of consequence to all peoples. In that recognition, The Cousteau Society asserted in late 1978 that a set of international principles should guide national initiatives so as to reinforce safeguards to a common heritage. Since, therefore, oceanic development requires a stewardship for future generations, any coastal bands under national jurisdiction should represent zones of long-term responsibility rather than of shorter term exploitation.

In contrast, the Law of the Sea negotiations have been largely bargaining sessions, propelled by parochial territorialism and perceptions of immediate national advantage. Connections have been neglected to foreign policy, to environmental management, to energy policy, to international trade and fiscal policy, to Third World development.

These issues have not been systematically examined, even in terms of longer run national self-interest, much less in terms of collective security. Also neglected is the fundamental reality that wise choices depend critically on new scientific information readily shared.

In years ahead, the evolving territorial agreements could well become part of the problem rather than of the solution.

To return to the broader issue, the rivalry between the United States and the USSR shows few signs of abatement. The numerous and articulate Third World independencies represent their views internally and externally as sovereign entities, reflecting diversity in culture, economic viability and national aspirations. Their demands for equality cannot be ignored.

All of these circumstances accelerate a new global consciousness. As one result, political processes may begin to differentiate global involvement from foreign policy,[160] with international problems beginning to be viewed as issues in human needs. Rather than as devils triggering ideological or military confrontations, conflicts could be perceived as unintended by-products of complexity, technological development and ignorance.

In the wake of this evolution, traditional compartments of domestic and foreign policy are now permeable because they are so interconnected. In the United States, for example, the undisciplined consumption of petroleum in a market free of domestic policy constraints required in 1978 the importation of 42 percent of its oil from foreign sources.

Not to be overlooked in these changing global affairs is the evolving importance of the multinational corporations, their role as transfer agent in intensive exploitation of technology, their power to circumvent or subvert intergovernmental relationships, but also their interest in promoting world order and relaxation of nationalistic constraints. The widespread uneasiness about multinationals stems from their relative immunity to public accountability. And in their invisibility they are free to exploit the paradox just mentioned of ballooning nationalism in the face of functional if not psychological obsolescence of nation-states as independent actors.

Some questions in global development have become keystones in studies of the future. In 1972, *Limits to Growth* was published. Taking the world as a whole, its authors claimed that because of physical limits to food, minerals, energy, industrial capacity and environmental resiliency, present trends were catastrophic. The study weathered storms of methodological criticism and spawned successors which refined the thesis and filled gaps. All suggested that hope lay only in restraint by international agreement, an anathema to the underdeveloped Third World that saw a conspiracy of continued bondage and delay of their self-realization. A more recent study by the University of Sussex[161] convincingly challenges the contention of physical limits, thus leaving to be investigated whether perhaps political limits may pose the ultimate dilemma. All, however, agree that the dimensions of the problem are global.

Basic Christian doctrine and proponents of world organization have been saying for a long time that we are all brothers on the same planet. A spate of institutional innovations, listed earlier, has been proposed as vehicles for this transformation. Elaboration of these prescriptions is beyond the scope of this book but certain implications earn comment.

If the United States is to tackle questions of its own survival, it cannot do it alone. It has, however, an enormously powerful fulcrum to elicit cooperation. For one thing, the United States has an unparalleled history of contributions to international interests. Unselfconsciously, it is both "the social pioneer and a guinea pig for mankind."[162] It has had a pervasive influence on other nations through both its spirit of freedom and its effervescent technological creativity. Other nations have been innocently helped toward their own futures by watching the United States wrestle, freely and openly, with its internal contradictions and dilemmas induced by technology.

If the United States should move deliberately to deal with questions of global survival, collaboration with other countries would be essential. While there are and may be for many years sharp differences in national views as to what people want, there is likely to be more universal and prompter agreement on what people do *not* want.

Survival of the species may be at stake, and only a community effort can assure it. An international convention has already been proposed dealing with social consequences of applied science and technology.[163] That concept could be greatly strengthened by moving from the abstract to the concrete as to its purpose.

Earlier, distinctions were drawn between two classes of neglect—

those emerging perils for which prophylactic action was weak, and those unwanted future consequences of current actions that were ignored for want of anticipatory interest and protective reaction. The human race may no longer be certain of survival, however it is organized politically, if it lacks common images of the future and a shared perception of mutual dangers. The earlier prescriptions advanced for Western nations have global counterparts.

It is on this latter point that there is a special opportunity for the Third World. From all the preceding discussion it is clear that technological progress of the West has triggered costly side effects. Yet technological engines must be employed in some degree and scale for liberation of the disadvantaged Third World from its curses.

From years of foreign technological assistance we have learned that simply pasting a veneer of technology onto a highly differentiated indigenous culture will not work. Mass export of the entire American setting is both unfeasible and immoral. What we need to recall, however, is that technology defined in a wide anthropological sense is an extremely important component of culture. It determines the relationship of a community with its natural environment, and is the most concrete expression of its values. "One of the main objectives of any process of deliberation by the developing countries should be to invest technology as one of the central energizing elements of their own unique cultural creativity."[164] So while Western technology in total is not an export commodity, certain techniques, if appropriate, may be.

What could be exported is a social process of anticipation. The reason is this. With developing nations having serious limits to human, natural and capital resources, they simply cannot afford waste or blunder. Also, transitions of technology require high sensitivity to matching technical resources congenially with social goals, infrastructure and processes. To avoid inadvertent and unwanted external costs puts a special premium on crisis-avoidance measures.[165] Technology assessment is one form of preventative medicine. Perhaps the greatest challenge is how to get the patient into the doctor's office: that is, how to inculcate an appetite for impact assessment, and for balancing long term consequences with perceived short term rewards.

There could well be an hospitable reception to such notions in developing countries. Broad social planning is widely practiced, especially in those engraved with procedural disciplines of military government. But under the impetus for swift achievements, actions are not ordinarily accompanied by the cautionary stance of looking ahead or sideways at consequences beyond the groove of project administration. The point is that there are lessons to be learned from the mistakes of the West, sins both of omission and commission in uncritically applying science and engineering. Given the thinly spread resources of Third World initiatives, the role of organized vigilance has a special meaning to reduce risk of their waste in resources due to high transaction costs, and frustration in reaching goals.

Technology transfer is the bland label for the "fix" by inoculation of developing nations with advanced science and engineering. That notion has been crippled by its interpretation of unidirectional flow. There are lessons that the West might learn *from* parts of the Third World, particularly cultural patterns bearing on the concept of time, the virtues of going slower. Clearly the West has no monopoly on social wisdom. Guaranteeing survival, with self-esteem, must be a partnership.

But to return to the central theme, all nations are in the same boat. If signals about the future are readable, credible and comprehensible, then all peoples must recognize that they are entering an era of unprecedented danger. For virtually all plausible hazards, the scale of calamity is such that it is unlikely there will be winners and losers; there will simply be (at best) survivors.

Such common perceptions gave rise in 1945 to creation of the United Nations for collective security. Its 30th birthday was celebrated on 24 October, 1975. But that anniversary was distinguished by feelings of cynicism over its role as a theater for developing nations to decry their historical deprivation rather than by ascendent hopes for the future by cooperative endeavors. To be sure, the U.N. system and its goals have been challenged by the parade of new members with equal voting rights. But the spirit has also been paradoxically damaged by its current preoccupation with accelerated economic development. On humanitarian grounds this focus can be lauded. But in accenting development, nationalistic tendencies for self-realization are fired up with blinding expectations of swift accomplishment, to the neglect of common threats.

Given the present inequities among the nation-states, development is an essential ingredient for conflict resolution, to reduce harsh disparities in wealth, economic vitality and social satisfactions. But development alone is *not* sufficient to see humankind through the next three decades. There must be collateral attention to survival. As The Cousteau Society has proposed, in dealing with the way ahead there must be a global Bill of Rights for future generations.

A program on a global scale would have the same ingredients as the prescriptions for one nation: vigilance, some liquidity in human, technical and fiscal resources, aids to education for the future, and public information. At the outset, these costs seem small. What this entails in deferred gratification is difficult to compute.

First, however, is a necessary international instrumentality to consider questions of survival, to plan and begin to act in harmony. Given that the initial steps are cultural and scientific, the existing United Nations Educational, Scientific and Cultural Organization would appear a candidate. Hopefully, this topic will not be neglected at the 1979 U.N. Conference on Science and Technology for Development. Their agenda might well add a new and portentous thrust for future generations on the planet, to be both alive and free.

CHAPTER 11

Epilogue

To Be Alive and Free, Rational Humanism Is Not Enough

For some 200 pages, reader and author have engaged in a vital but deeply troubling enterprise—probing the circumstances of human survival. The author had two primary intentions: first, to serve as navigator rather than sage in exploring sources of the current predicament; and, second, to provoke a stronger personal commitment by the reader to ask questions and consider arguments advanced as to why the policy apparatus we depend on for steering in perilous seas acts as if it were deaf to signals about the future. While skipping detail and granting inevitable limitations of scholarship, experience and judgment, the author has endeavored to share everything he thinks he may know. But having shared that essence of reason, he hopes to have earned the interest and confidence of the reader sufficiently to go one further brief step—to share how he feels.

This does not mean submitting a report card on unrelenting gloom about the end of the world nor a balance sheet of villains and heroes. Rather, there is distilled a purely intuitive essence on where we stand and what else we must do.

To the author survival means life, but life with freedom, self-esteem and dignity. Moreover, it is a life ennobled by science. Indeed, science and technology have afforded for hundreds of millions a new scale of human freedoms—freedom from poverty and despair, from backbreaking labor, disability and disease, from ignorance, from limitations of geography and environment.

The unnerving counterpoint to this beneficence is found in unwanted side effects. Consequences arise from uncritical applications of science and technology, ignorance and error, and they wax more swiftly and more ominously than countermeasures can be introduced. The next 20 years are ones of great danger. The blame, however, cannot be placed on a mindless technology. Nor can it be ascribed simply to weak political leadership. Given our manifest loss of control, the malfunctions lie in institutions we hold responsible for guidance of technology. And their ineptness in anticipation reveals an unwitting surrender to pathologies of the short run. Moreover, these pathologies rooted in our culture shackle and undermine our entire political decision system.

Although both technology and public policy may be designed for short run performance, both inevitably cast shadows ahead. Thus, a concern for nimble and sensitive political steering to avoid calamity must take the future into fundamental account. Widespread experience with both technology and public policy teaches us that the present host of life-threatening dilemmas was seeded yesterday. Those of tomorrow, even more poignant and potentially lethal, are sure to be nurtured by decisions today. So we are challenged to act with wisdom now to head off those scenarios we do not want.

Taking the future into account brings to mind that the future is not what it used to be. Founding fathers of the United States saw the future as almost completely open, open to geographical occupation and conquest of the wilderness, to economic growth reinforced by powerful technological engines, to individual initiative, to ultimate perfectability of democratic institutions. That future is now constrained. There are limits to space and natural resources; and limits to individual autonomy. The author, however, rejects any notion that the future is closed, only that in secular terms it is for the first time bounded for everyone on the planet. That may be a heavy psychological burden for some to accept. But it is not cause for despair.

These constraints may be temporary. No one knows for sure. They certainly need not crush the human spirit because of the boundless opportunities for creativity, discovery, diversity and inner fulfillment.

Nevertheless, to enjoy life, we must have life and it is survival that is at stake, survival of the human race that requires new social learning, and soon.

The diagnosis of political acoustics led to prescriptions enabling survival. They explicitly call for a change in behavior by every sector in our technological world, a set of interlocking reforms in anticipation and common commitment to collective security if we are to have a future at all.

History teaches us that people do mobilize their energies toward common goals. Various national developments, including the United States, provide glowing examples. Yet, such mobilizations are most graphically dramatized in times of military threat to a preferred way of life. Today, we must reconsider the futures we do not want in order to have those we do. In the absence of a clear and present danger, we may be experiencing an era without a cause.

Yet the heart of the matter lies in our proclivity to fasten on the short run, in Western society, with hedonistic abandon. We seem to have spun a cultural web where the predilection for the short run may constitute a self-fulfilling prophecy that by benign neglect of the longer run, there may be none. To herald economic growth as an end in itself, to acquire the fashionable and popular symbols of contemporary existence, to focus only on living and being, and to abdicate personal responsibility to government or third-party institutions, reflect a melancholy fact that we have neglected a higher order of social guidance; we have abandoned a moral hierarchy.

A hint as to the author's feelings was offered earlier in the section on people and personhood, on the desperate importance of human capacity for compassion and love, on the positive regard for truth and honor, on survival value in nonmanipulative, nonexploitive conduct. Far from being new canons of behavior, these have bubbled to the surface of all cultures over thousands of years. They have not, however, proved enduring.

From history we know about cycles of ennui to élan in conjecture about the way ahead. That cultural idealism has periodically surfaced as a boon to survival, however, lends credence to the energy of moral imperative in human existence. Assuming that a consensus develops for a restatement of moral commitment, can a cultural modification occur in time?

It is in that context that the author fastens on one central theme as a compass for the future—an acceptance of the role of religion. But it is religion for today, not a religion rooted in cultural models and earlier-day challenges to personal existence. The church may be our only institution devoted to a collective redemption in the future; it is basically not one of the functional components of the technological delivery system. To the contrary, it is fundamentally committed to spiritual dimensions of eternity, and of grace. Of all our institutions, only it has the capacity to set the stage of individual behavior from which all participants may take sustenance of shared images: images of person, images of reality and images of the future.

This is neither a passive role nor a flaccid responsibility. To overcome the reluctance or even shame of passionate moral indignation, what may be needed, to use George Steiner's phrase, is an "ecstatic rage" for truth and justice, a quest for perfection and for fulfillment of human possibilities, the willingness to sacrifice, the humility of admitting the Divine in our lives. This is not to be found in education or educational institutions, or even in the sometimes vain enterprise of knowledge production. Neither the new technological equipment nor the technologically based social organizations have spurred constant dedication to humane social conduct, collective serenity or responsibility of transmitting the inheritance of life as a legacy to be honored, enriched and conserved.

The greatest irony is the almost universal propensity in life-threatening situations for individuals of all shades and degrees of belief to call on God for help.

Alexander Solzhenitsyn in his commencement address at Harvard University in June 1978 makes this author's case with the advantage of profound insight and historical perspective. In charging the Western world with loss in courage and spiritual direction, he recalled that in democracy freedom was given to the individual conditionally, in "the assumption of his constant religious responsibility." But in having lost the "concept of a Supreme Complete Entity which used to restrain our passions . . . we have placed too much hope in political and social reforms, only to find that we were being deprived of our most precious possession: our spiritual life." Continues Solzhenitsyn, man's task cannot be unrestrained enjoyment of everyday life and the search for the best ways to obtain material goods. Rather, it has to be fulfillment of a permanent, earnest duty to leave life better than when one first encountered it. And this requires voluntary, inspired self-restraint. "Our lives will have to change if we want to save life from self-destruction . . . no one on earth has any other way left but upward."

Whatever the unsettling effects of technologically pulsed change, there must be a renewed definition of cardinal aids to survival—those immutable values that light the way.

Only by such illumination may we hope for victories over doomsday.

References

1. Michael Marien, *Societal Directions and Alternatives* (LaFayette, New York: Information for Policy Design, 1976), p. 15.
2. Karl W. Deutsch, *Nationalism and its Alternatives* (New York: Knopf, 1969).
3. Richard A. Falk, *A Study of Future Worlds* (New York: The Free Press, 1975), ch. III.
4. Daniel Bell, *The Coming of Post-Industrial Society: A Venture in Social Forecasting* (New York: Basic Books, 1973).
5. George Steiner, *In Bluebeard's Castle: Some Notes Toward the Redefinition of Culture* (New Haven: Yale Univ. Press, 1973), p. 69.
6. Donella H. Meadows, Dennis L. Meadows, Jorgen Randers and William W. Behrens III, *The Limits to Growth: A Report for the Club of Rome's Project on the Predicament of Mankind* (New York: Universe Books, 1972). Robert L. Heilbroner, *An Inquiry into the Human Prospect* (New York: Norton, 1974). Roberto Vacca, *The Coming Dark Age* (Garden City, New York: Doubleday, 1973). Rufus E. Miles, *Awakening from the American Dream* (New York: Universe, 1976). Gordon Rattray Taylor, *How to Avoid the Future* (London: Secker & Warburg, 1975). H. G. Wells, *World Brain* (Freeport, New York: Books for Libraries Press, 1971).
7. Daniel Bell, *Post-Industrial Society.*
8. John Kenneth Galbraith, *The New Industrial State* (Boston: Houghton Mifflin, 1967).
9. Elise Boulding, "Futurology and the Capacity of the West" in *Search for Alternatives: Public Policy and the Study of the Future,* Franklin Tugwell, ed. (Cambridge: Winthrop, 1973).
10. George Steiner, *In Bluebeard's Castle,* p. 70.
11. National Research Council, *Long-term Worldwide Effects of Multiple Nuclear Weapons Detonations* (Washington: NAS, 1975). Kenneth E. Boulding, *The Meaning of the Twentieth Century: The Great Transition* (New York: Harper & Row, 1964), p. 80.
12. Georg Borgstrom, *Food—The Great Challenge of the Century* (New York: Universe Books, 1976). Michael Jacobson, *Food for People Not for Profit* (New York: Ballantine, 1975). Lester R. Brown and Erik P. Eckholm, *By Bread Alone* (New York: Praeger, 1974). National Research Council, *World Food and Nutrition Study* (Washington: NAS, 1975).
13. William Murdoch, ed., *Environment* (Stanford, Conn.: Sinauer Assoc., 1972). National Research Council, *Assessing Potential Ocean Pollutants* (Washington:

NAS, 1975). S. Fred Singer, ed., *Global Effects of Environmental Pollution* (New York: Springer-Verlag, 1970).

14. Edward Goldsmith, "Blueprint for Survival," *The Ecologist*, II, No. 1 (1972). U.S. President, Council on Environmental Quality, *Fifth Annual Report* (Washington: GPO, 1974).
15. Stephen H. Schneider, *The Genesis Strategy—Climate and Global Survival* (New York: Plenum Press, 1976). Stephen H. Schneider and W. W. Kellogg, *Science*, No. 186 (27 Dec. 1974), pp. 1163–1167. W. C. Wang, *Science*, No. 194 (12 Nov. 1976), pp. 685–695. "Study of Man's Impact on Climate (SMIC)," *Inadvertent Climate Modification* (Cambridge, Mass.: MIT Press, 1971). Paul E. Dumar and Steven M. Kunen, "Global Cooling," *Science*, No. 193 (6 Aug. 1976), pp. 447–457. Helmut Landsberg and Lester Machta, *Ambio*, Vol. III, No. 3 (1974), p. 146. National Research Council, *Climate, Climatic Change and Water Supply* (Washington: NAS, 1977). U. Siegenthaler and H. Oeschger, "Predicting Future Atmospheric Carbon Dioxide Levels," *Science*, Vol. 199, No. 4327 (1978), pp. 388–395.
16. Mark Kasoff, "Cities on the Brink: New York and Others," *Antioch Review*, Winter, 1977. Alan Altshuler, "The Politics of Urban Transportation Innovation," *Technology Review* (May, 1977), pp. 51–58.
17. *New York Times* (12 Jan. 1977, 1:2).
18. Meadows, *et al., The Limits to Growth*. Carroll Wilson, ed., *Energy: Global Prospects, 1985–2000* (Cambridge, Mass.: MIT Press, 1977). National Academy of Sciences, *Energy: Future Alternatives and Risks* (Cambridge, Mass.: Ballinger, 1974). Harrison Brown, "Resource Needs and Demands," in *Notes for the Future*, Robin Claude, ed. (New York: Universe Books, 1976). National Research Council, *Resources and Man: A Study and Recommendations in Pollution, Resources and the Environment* (New York: W. W. Norton, 1973).
19. National Academy of Engineering, Committee on Public Engineering Policy, *Research Applicable to National Needs* (Washington: NAS, 1972).
20. Bertram M. Gross, "Friendly Fascism: A Model for America," *Social Policy*, 1:4 (Nov./Dec. 1970), pp. 287–301. Edgar Z. Friedenberg, *The Disposal of Liberty and Other Industrial Wastes* (New York: Doubleday, 1975). *New York Times* (13 March, 1977, 1:6). Harold Lasswell, "The Garrison State," *American Journal of Sociology*, Jan. 1941.
21. C. Reznikoff, *Holocaust* (Los Angeles: Black Sparrow Press, 1975). Richard M. Restak, *Premeditated Man: Bioethics and the Control of Future Human Life* (New York: Viking, 1975). S. N. Cohen, "Recombinant DNA: Fact and Fiction," *Science*, Vol. 195, No. 4279, pp. 654–657. Clifford Grobstein, "The Recombinant DNA Debate," *Scientific American*, Vol. 237, No. 1 (July 1977), pp. 23–33. George Wald, "Genetic Engineering: The Case Against Genetic Engineering," *Curent*, 187: 25–30 (Nov. 1976).
22. Kenneth E. Boulding, *The Meaning of the Twentieth Century: The Great Transition* (New York: Harper & Row, 1964), p. 80.
23. John Platt, "What We Must Do," *Science*, 166 (28 Nov., 1969), pp. 1115–1121.
24. Mason Willrich and Theodore B. Taylor, *Nuclear Theft: Risks and Safeguards* (Cambridge: Ballinger, 1974).
25. John Platt, "What We Must Do".
26. William O. Lowrance, *Of Acceptable Risk—Science and Determination of Safety*

(Los Altos: William Kaufmann, Inc., 1976), p. 8. National Academy of Engineering, *Perspectives on Benefit–Risk Decision Making*, NAE Committee on Public Engineering Policy, Washington, DC, 1972, 157 pp.
27. Kenneth M. Dolbeare, "The Impact of Public Policy," *Political Science Annual* (New York: Bobbs Merrill, 1973).
28. Harold K. Jacobson and Eric Stein, *Diplomats, Scientists and Politicians—The United States and the Nuclear Test Ban Negotiations* (Ann Arbor: Univ. of Michigan Press, 1966).
29. R. V. Jones, *The Wizard War—British Scientific Intelligence in 1939–1945* (New York: Coward, McCann and Geoghegan, Inc., 1978). William Stevenson, *A Man Called Intrepid* (New York: Ballantine, 1976). Ronald W. Clark, *The Birth of the Bomb* (London: Phoenix House, Ltd., 1961). Graham Allison, *Essence of Decision: Explaining the Cuban Missile Crisis* (Boston: Little, Brown & Co., 1971).
30. Zbigniew Brzezinski, *Between Two Ages: America's Role in the Technetronic Era* (New York: Viking, 1970), p. 106.
31. Alexander Solzhenitsyn, *From Under the Rubble* (New York: Little, Brown & Co., 1975).
32. R. A. Caro, *The Power Broker: Robert Moses and the Fall of New York* (New York: Vintage, 1975).
33. Edward Wenk, Jr., "SST—Implications of a Political Decision," *Astronautics and Aeronautics*, 9 (Oct. 1971), pp. 40–49.
34. John Costello and Terry Hughes, *The Concorde Conspiracy—The International Race for the SST* (New York: Charles Scribner's Sons, 1976).
35. Alvin Toffler, *Future Shock* (New York: Random House, 1970).
36. Geoffrey Vickers, *Freedom in a Rocking Boat: Changing Values in an Unstable Society* (London: Allen Lane, Penguin, 1970).
37. Elliot Richardson, *The Creative Balance: A Post-Watergate Look at the American People and Politics* (New York: Holt, Rinehart & Winston, 1976).
38. Hazel Henderson, "Ideologies, Paradigms and Myths: Changes in our Operative Social Values," *Liberal Education*, May 1976, Vol. LXII, No. 2, pp. 143–177. ——*Creating Alternative Futures: The End of Economics* (New York: Berkeley Publishing Co., 1978).
39. Robert M. Pirsig, *Zen and the Art of Motorcycle Maintenance* (New York: William Morrow & Co., Inc., 1974).
40. Edward Wenk, Jr., "Social Management of Technology," *Science for Society*, John E. Mock, ed., Proceedings of the National Science Conference, Atlanta, Oct. 1970, pp. 8–31.
41. John Kenneth Galbraith, *The New Industrial State*.
42. Bertram M. Gross, "The State of the Nation: Social Systems Accounting," Raymond Bauer, ed., *Social Indicators* (Cambridge, Mass.: MIT Press, 1966), pp. 183–184.
43. Hazel Henderson, "Ideologies, Paradigms and Myths".
44. Sam Love, "The Overconnected Society," *The Futurist*, 8:6, Dec. 1974, pp. 293–295.
45. Geoffrey Vickers, *Value Systems and Social Process* (London: Tavistock, 1968), p. 42.
46. Karl W. Deutsch, *The Nerves of Government* (New York: The Free Press, 1963), p. 219.
47. Ibid.

48. Edward Wenk, Jr., *The Politics of the Oceans* (Seattle: Univ. of Washington Press, 1972), p. 382.
49. Karl W. Deutsch, *The Nerves of Government*, p. 92. See also, C. West Churchman, *The Design of Inquiring Systems* (New York: Basic Books, 1971). David Easton, *A Systems Analysis of Political Life* (New York: Wiley, 1965). Harold L. Wilensky, *Organizational Intelligence* (New York: Basic Books, 1967). Ida Hoos, *Systems Analysis in Public Policy* (Berkeley: Univ. of California Press, 1972). Amitai Etzioni, *A Sociological Reader on Complex Organizations* (New York: Holt, Rinehart & Winston, 1969). Erich Jantsch, *Design for Evolution* (New York: George Braziller, 1975).
50. Edward Wenk, Jr. and Thomas J. Kuehn, "Interinstitutional Networks in Technological Delivery Systems," in *Science and Technology Policy*, Joseph Haberer, ed. (Lexington, Mass.: D. C. Heath, 1977).
51. Jay D. Starling, "The Use of System Constraints in Simplifying Organized Social Complexity," in *Organized Social Complexity—Challenge to Politics and Policy*, Todd R. LaPorte, ed. (Princeton: Princeton Univ. Press, 1975), p. 181.
52. Charles Lindblom, "The Science of Muddling Through," *PAR* 19 (1959), pp. 79–88.
53. Irving L. Janis and Leon Mann, "Coping with Decisional Stress," *American Scientist*, Vol. 64, pp. 657–667.
54. Milton Katz, mentioned in private communication, Harvard University, 18 Oct., 1976.
55. Walter Lippmann, "Today and Tomorrow—Catching up with the Times," *Washington Post*, 14 Nov., 1966.
56. Geoffrey Vickers, *Freedom in a Rocking Boat*, p. 43.
57. Donald N. Michael, *The Unprepared Society: Planning for a Precarious Future* (New York: Basic Books, 1968).
58. Herbert A. Simon, "The Architecture of Complexity," *Proceedings of the American Philosophical Society*, 106 (1962).
59. Todd R. LaPorte, ed., *Organized Social Complexity—Challenge to Politics and Policy* (Princeton: Princeton Univ. Press, 1975), p. 19. Also chapter by Langdar Winner, "Complexity and the Limits of Human Understanding" and by J. Serge Taylor on "Organizational Complexity in the New Industrial State—The Role of Technology".
60. John Gerard Rugge, "Complexity, Planning and Public Order" in Todd R. LaPorte.
61. Ibid.; also Garry D. Brewer, "An Analysis of Complex Systems" in Todd R. LaPorte.
62. Jay D. Starling, "The Use of System Constraints in Simplifying Organized Social Complexity" in Todd R. LaPorte.
63. Donald N. Michael, *The Unprepared Society: Planning for a Precarious Future*, p. 7.
64. Ibid., p. 86; also Geoffrey Vickers, *The Art of Judgment* (New York: Basic Books, 1965), p. 81.
65. Warren Wagar, *Building the City of Man: Outlines of a World Civilization* (New York: Grossman, 1971).
66. Z. Brzezinski, *Between Two Ages*, p. 76.
67. Peter Drucker, *The Age of Discontinuity* (New York: Harper & Row, 1969), p. 194.

68. Graham Allison, *Essence of Decision: Explaining the Cuban Missile Crisis* (Boston: Little, Brown & Co., 1971).
69. Kenneth Boulding, *The Image* (Ann Arbor: Univ. of Michigan Press, 1971), pp. 64, 125.
70. Fred Polak, *The Image of the Future*, translated and abridged by Elise Boulding (San Francisco: Jossey Bass/Elsevier, 1973).
71. Charles L. Sanford, *The Quest for Paradise* (Urbana: Univ. of Illinois Press, 1961).
72. Thomas William Sine, Jr., "Images of the Future in the American Past: Visions for Education." Unpublished Ph.D. dissertation, University of Washington, Seattle, 1978.
73. Geoffrey Vickers, *Freedom in a Rocking Boat*, p. 20.
74. E. C. Zeeman, "Catastrophe Theory," *Scientific American*, April 1976, pp. 65–83.
75. Franklin Ingwell, ed., *Search for Alternatives: Public Policy and the Study of the Future* (Cambridge: Winthrop, 1973), p. vi.
76. Elise Boulding, *Futurology and the Capacity of the West.*
77. Harold Lasswell, *The Policy Sciences—Recent Developments in Scope and Methods* (Palo Alto: Stanford Univ. Press, 1951).
78. C. P. Snow, "What is the World's Greatest Need?" *N.Y. Times Magazine*, 2 April, 1961.
79. Rufus E. Miles, *Awakening from the American Dream.*
80. Geoffrey Vickers, *Value Systems and Social Process*, p. 50.
81. Peter Marris, *Loss and Change* (New York: Pantheon, 1974), p. 170.
82. Michael Marien, *Societal Directions and Alternatives.*
83. Leo Szilard, *The Voice of the Dolphin* (New York: Simon & Schuster, 1961), pp. 25–26.
84. Public Law 94–282.
85. *New Yorker*, editorial, 8 July, 1974, pp. 25–26.
86. Harold D. Lasswell and Daniel Lerner, eds., *The Policy Sciences—Recent Developments in Scope and Methods* (Stanford: Stanford Univ. Press, 1951).
87. Charles Galton Darwin, *The Next Million Years* (Garden City, New York: Doubleday & Co., 1953). Aldous Huxley, *Brave New World Revisited* (New York: Harper Bros., 1958).
88. Margaret Mead, *Culture and Commitment: A Study of the Generation Gap* (New York: Doubleday & Co., 1970).
89. Bertram M. Gross, "Friendly Fascism: A Model for America," *Social Policy* 1: 4, (Nov./Dec. 1970), pp. 287–301.
90. Theodore Roszak, *Where the Wasteland Ends: Politics and Transcendence in Post-Industrial Society* (Garden City, New York: Doubleday & Co., 1972), p. 417.
91. Herbert Hendin, *The Age of Sensation* (New York: Norton, 1975), p. 334.
92. *Time Magazine*, 14 Nov., 1977.
93. Bertrand Russell, *In Praise of Idleness* (New York: W. W. Norton & Co., 1935), p. 18.
94. Walter Kerr, *The Decline of Pleasure* (New York: Simon & Schuster, 1965), p. 39.
95. Staffan Burenstam Linder, *The Harried Leisure Class* (New York: Columbia Univ. Press, 1970).
96. Herbert A. Simon, "Theories of Decision Making in Economics and Behavioral Science," *American Economic Review*, June 1959, pp. 253–283.
97. J. Hanrahan and O. Gruenstein, *Lost Frontier: The Marketing of Alaska* (New York: W. W. Norton, 1977), pp. 123–175. M. C. Berry, *The Alaska Pipeline: The*

Politics of Oil and Native Land Claims (Bloomington, Ind.: Indiana Univ. Press, 1975).

98. Deborah Shapley, review of *Advice and Dissent* by Joel Primack and Frank van Hippel, *New York Times*, Book Review (29 June, 1975).
99. U.S. House of Representatives, *The Office of Science and Technology*, Edward Wenk, Jr., ed., Committee on Government Operations (Washington: GPO, 1967). C. E. Barfield, "White House Office Abolished," *National Journal*, Vol. 5, No. 5 (1973), pp. 158–159.
100. National Academy of Sciences, *Science and Technology in Presidential Policy-making—A Proposal*, report of the ad hoc Committee on Science and Technology (Washington, NAS, June 1974), 56 pp.
101. U.S. Senate, *Testimony by Edward Wenk, Jr. on S. 2495*, "Science and Technology Applications Act of 1974" before the Commerce and Aeronautical and Space Sciences Committee, 93rd Congress, 11 July, 1974. U.S. Senate, *Statement by Edward Wenk, Jr.* before the Labor and Public Welfare Committee, 8 Oct., 1974.
102. Amitai Etzioni, "Social Science in the White House," editorial in *Science*, Vol. 194, No. 4270, 10 Dec., 1976, p. 1119.
103. American Society for Public Administration, *Resolution in Support of Principles for Technology Policy Advice to the President*, adopted Chicago, Ill., Spring Meeting, 1975.
104. U.S. House of Representatives, *Statement by Edward Wenk, Jr. on Federal Policy, Plans and Organization for Science and Technology II* before the Science and Astronautics Committee, Oct. 1974.
105. National Goals Research Staff, *Towards Balanced Growth: Quantity with Quality* (Washington: GPO, 1970).
106. Roberto Vacca, *The Coming Dark Age*.
107. Rufus E. Miles, *Awakening from the American Dream*.
108. Jay W. Forrester, *World Dynamics* (Cambridge, Mass.: Wright Allen, 1971).
109. Robert L. Heilbroner, *An Inquiry into the Human Prospect*.
110. Z. Brzezinski, *Between Two Ages*, p. xiv.
111. E. E. Schumaker, *Small is Beautiful—Economics as if People Mattered* (New York: Harper & Row, 1973).
112. Charles Reich, *The Greening of America* (New York: Random House, 1970).
113. Kenneth E. Boulding, *The Meaning of the Twentieth Century*.
114. John Platt, "What We Must Do".
115. Geoffrey Vickers, *Value Systems and Social Process*, p. vi.
116. Elliot Richardson, *The Creative Balance*.
117. Hazel Henderson, *Ideologies, Paradigms and Myths*.
118. Thomas S. Kuhn, *The Structure of the Scientific Revolution* (Chicago: Univ. of Chicago Press, 1962).
119. Geoffrey Vickers, *Value Systems and Social Process*, p. 159.
120. John Platt, book reviews, *Science*, Vol. 80, 11 May, 1973, pp. 580–582.
121. James D. Carroll, "Participatory Technology," *Science*, Vol. 171, No. 3972, pp. 647–653.
122. Citizens Task Force, *Alternatives for Washington*, Vol. VII, Office of Program Planning and Fiscal Management, State Planning Division, State of Washington, Nov. 1976. Royal Ministry for Foreign Affairs (Sweden), *To Choose a Future*, (Secretariat for Future Studies, Stockholm, 1974).

123. Luther P. Gerlach and Virginia H. Hine, *Lifeway Leap* (Minneapolis: Univ. of Minnesota Press, 1973).
124. Gordon Rattray Taylor, *Rethink: A Paraprimitive Solution* (New York: E. P. Dutton, 1973), p. 165.
125. John Dewey, *The Quest for Certainty* (New York: G. P. Putnam & Sons, 1939), p. 37.
126. George Steiner, *In Bluebeard's Castle*, p. 133.
127. Alvin Toffler, *Learning for Tomorrow* (New York: Random House, 1974), p. 3.
128. Aldous Huxley, *Brave New World Revisited* (London: Chatto & Windus, 1959), p. 73.
129. Vannever Bush, *Science—The Endless Frontier*.
130. George Steiner, *In Bluebeard's Castle*, p. 138.
131. Don K. Price, *The Scientific Estate* (Cambridge: Harvard Univ. Press, 1965).
132. Harvey Brooks in *Basic Research and National Goals*, Report to Committee on Science and Astronautics, U.S. House of Representatives, 89th Congress, 1st Session (Washington: NAS, 1965), pp. 77–110.
133. J. Huizinga, *In the Shadow of Tomorrow* (New York: W. W. Norton, 1936), p. 79.
134. Donald N. Michael, *The Unprepared Society*, p. 78.
135. Edward Wenk, Jr., "Engineering, A Profession for the Future," *The Bent*, Tau Beta Pi, Spring, 1978.
136. William Bevan, "The Sound of the Wind That's Blowing," *American Psychologist*, Vol. 32, No. 7 (July 1976), pp. 481–491; with excellent bibliography.
137. Arthur Kantrowitz, "Proposal for an Institution for Scientific Judgment," *Science*, Vol. 156, No. 3776 (1967), pp. 763–764.
138. Barry M. Casper, "Technology Policy and Democracy—Is the Proposed Science Court What We Need?" *Science*, 194 (1 Oct., 1976), pp. 29–35. Arthur Kantrowitz, "The Science Court Experiments: Criticisms and Responses," *Bulletin of the Atomic Scientists* (April 1977), pp. 44–53; "Controlling Technology Democratically," *American Scientist* 63, 505 (1975).
139. Z. Brzezinski, "The American Transition," *The New Republic*, 23 Dec., 1967, pp. 18–21.
140. Stuart Chase, *The Most Probable World* (New York: Harper & Row, 1968), p. 209.
141. Alvin Toffler, *Future Shock*.
142. Donella H. Meadows, Dennis L. Meadows, Jorgen Randers and William W. Behrens III, *The Limits to Growth*.
143. Joseph A. Califano, Jr., *A Presidential Nation* (New York: W. W. Norton, 1975).
144. Edward Wenk, Jr., *The Politics of the Oceans*, pp. 544–545.
145. Joseph F. Coates, "Some Methods and Techniques for Comprehensive Impact Assessments," *Technological Forecasting and Social Change*, Vol. VI, 1974, pp. 341–357.
146. Edward Wenk, Jr., "Social Management of Technology."
147. Eugene B. Skolnikoff, "The Office of Technology Assessment," in *Congressional Support Agencies: A Compilation of Papers*, Commission on the Operation of the Senate (Washington: GPO, 1976), pp. 55–74. U.S. House of Representatives, Commission on Information and Facilities, *The Office of Technology Assessment: A Study of the Organizational Effectiveness* (Washington: GPO, 1977).
148. U.S. House of Representatives, *Statement by Edward Wenk, Jr.* concerning *The*

Office of Technology Assessment, before the Subcommittee on Science, Research and Technology, 19 Oct., 1977.

149. Michael Harrington, *Towards a Democratic Left: A Radical Program for a New Majority* (New York: Macmillan, 1968).
150. Edward Wenk, Jr., "Technology Assessment: Concepts, Practice and Experience in the United States," presented at the Workshop on Technology Assessment, Canberra, Australia, 3 July, 1978.
151. Amitai Etzioni, *The Active Society—A Theory of Societal and Political Processes* (New York: The Free Press, 1968), p. 480.
152. Nicholas E. Golovin, "The Evaluative Function in Government" in *Cybernetics and the Management of Large Systems*, E. M. Dewan, ed. (New York: Spartan Books, 1969), pp. 157–187.
153. U.S. House of Representatives, *Statement by Edward Wenk, Jr.* concerning *The Office of Technology Assessment*, before the Subcommittee on Science, Research, and Development, June, 1970.
154. Karl W. Deutsch, "On the Learning Capacity of Large Political Systems" in *Information for Action: From Knowledge to Wisdom* (New York: Academic Press, 1975), pp. 61–83.
155. James G. Miller, "Living Systems: The Organization," *Behavioral Sciences*, Vol. 17, 1972, pp. 1–182.
156. S. 3202 94th Congress introduced by Senator Edward M. Kennedy, *Congressional Quarterly Almanac*, 94th Congress, 2nd Session, Vol. 32 (1976), pp. 596–599.
157. John W. Gardner, *The Recovery of Confidence* (New York: W. W. Norton, 1970).
158. Geoffrey Vickers, *Art of Judgment, A Study of Policy Making* (New York: Basic Books, 1965), p. 87.
159. Z. Brzezinski, *Between Two Ages*, p. 307.
160. Ibid.
161. Christopher Freeman and M. Jahoda, eds., *World Futures: The Great Debate* (Sussex: Science Policy Research Unit, University of Sussex, 1978).
162. Z. Brzezinski, *Between Two Ages*, p. xv.
163. Ibid., p. 300.
164. Solomon Encel, Pauline K. Marston and William Page, *Art of Anticipation—Values and Methods in Forecasting* (London: Martin Robertson, 1975), p. 236.
165. M. Joghi Farvar and John P. Milton, *The Careless Technology, Ecology and International Development* (Garden City, New York: Natural History Press, 1972).

Index

HIRAM COLLEGE